DURHAM CITY
The Ultimate Collection
1935-1950   Vol.1

DURHAM CITY
The Ultimate Collection
1935-1950   Vol. 1

MICHAEL RICHARDSON

This edition published in Great Britain in 2017
by DB Publishing, an imprint of JMD Media Ltd

© Michael Richardson, 2017

All Rights Reserved. No part of this publication may be reproduced, stored in a retrieval system, or transmitted in any form, or by any means, electronic, mechanical, photocopying, recording or otherwise without the prior permission in writing of the copyright holders, nor be otherwise circulated in any form or binding or cover other than in which it is published and without a similar condition being imposed on the subsequent publisher.

ISBN 978-1-78091-565-4

Printed and bound in the UK

Contents

Introduction	7
Acknowledgements	8
1935	**9**
27 July 1935 - Miners' Gala	15
1936	**26**
25 July 1936 - Miners' Gala	41
1937	**46**
24 July 1937 - Miners' Gala	58
1938	**65**
23 July 1938 - Miners' Gala	78
1939	**88**
22 July 1939 - Miners' Gala	98
1940	**105**
1941	**109**
1942	**115**
1946	**117**
20 July 1946 - Miners' Gala	125
1947	**134**
26 July 1947 - Miners' Gala	148
1948	**161**
24 July 1948 - Miners' Gala	172
1949	**178**
23 July 1949 - Miners' Gala	189
1950	**203**
22 July 1950 - Miners' Gala	214

Introduction

This collection of photographs has been brought together to cover a specific period of life, in and around Durham City, from 1935 to 1950. This is the first time that such a comprehensive collection has been put together. The book is laid out in chronological order beginning with a fine portrait of Durham's oldest Freeman, Mr John Vest, aged 90, of Pity Me. There are numerous sporting photographs throughout, which show the strong link Durham people have had with competitive sports. The student 'Rag', once one of the highlights in the Durham calendar, is well-covered. The Silver Link Bridge, linking Gilesgate to Pelaw Wood, is seen on the day of its opening, 12 April 1938. As we get to 1939 many of the photographs show preparations under way, for the beginning of World War Two – gas mask drills, Land Army training at Houghall and air raid precautions exercises. It is noticeable that the Durham Ice Rink has played an important role in the leisure life of Durham people. Because of World War Two, there was a shortage of photographs, especially the years 1943–45, due the limited supply of film (If any reader has photographs from this period, I would very much like to hear from them). After the war, in October 1947, Mr Tilly is photographed showing German prisoners-of-war around Durham Cathedral. The same POW's returned to the cathedral in December that year to present gifts of toys to be placed under the Christmas tree. The 1st Battalion Durham Light Infantry's departure for Korea is captured. It is seen marching into the city for a special farewell service in the cathedral. In May 2002, the Queen, as part of her Golden Jubilee celebrations, visited Durham City. Her first visit to the city was in October 1947.

On 20 November 1869 the first meeting of the Durham Miners' Association was held in the Market Hotel, Durham Market Place. Two years later, on 12 August 1871, 5,000 miners and their families converged upon the city for their first 'Big Meeting'. The venue was Wharton Park, which had been loaned for the occasion by John Lloyd Wharton, MP. The following year it was held on The Racecourse where it has been held ever since, except for the following years: 1915-18, 1921, 1922, 1926 and 1940-45. The 'Big Meeting' was a day of pageantry when the miners entered the city, like the victors of a great battle, with banners held high. These images brings alive the memories of those who were involved with this special day and enlightens those who never knew it at its peak. They show the strong community spirit of the people of the Durham coalfield. . A poignant reminder of the casualties each year was the many banners draped in black.

If you have had connections with the city between 1935 to 1950, you will almost certainly recognise familiar faces here. If you have had no connections, then this volume will help to explain why Durham City is such a special place. However this is a good time for me to stop, and for you to look at the photographic treasures this volume contains.

Michael Richardson 2017

Acknowledgements

So many people have donated and loaned photographs to the Gilesgate Archive, that it is impossible to thank them all individually. Special thanks go to: Mr F. Bilton, Major R.S. Cross, Mr I. Forsyth, Mr G. Gilson, Mr J. Harrop, Mr R. Hopps, Mr C. Lloyd, Mr G. Marley, Miss D.M. Meade, Mr Billy Mollon, Mr G.R.S. Nelson, Mr R. Norris, Miss E. Richardson, Mrs N. Richardson, Dr C.D. Watkinson and Mr D. Young. The staff of the following institutions have helped in various ways: Durham University Library, the Dean and Chapter Library, Durham Clayport Library, Durham Record Office and The History of Durham Project.

1935

Durham's oldest Freeman, Mr John Vest, on his 90th birthday, photographed on 3 January 1935. He lived at Pity Me and his good health enabled him to visit Durham City every week.

The man with the 'coldest job' in the city, a stonemason working on scaffolding at the topmost walls of Durham Castle, January 1935. Note the wooden poles fastened together with rope.

Mrs Susan Kingston, centre, a grand old lady of 83, enjoying teatime treats given by Bearpark WI at the Colliery Institute for the over 65s, 8 January 1935. She was the mother of Alderman W. Kingston of Bearpark. After tea entertainment was provided by pupils of Miss Lillian Ainsley's dancing school of Durham. Men were given an ounce of tobacco and ladies half a pound of tea.

The new building belonging to Mackay's carpet factory, April 1935. The cottages on the right were later demolished to make room for the ice-rink. The green area is the Durham County Girls' School playing field (now the site of Durham's new swimming baths).

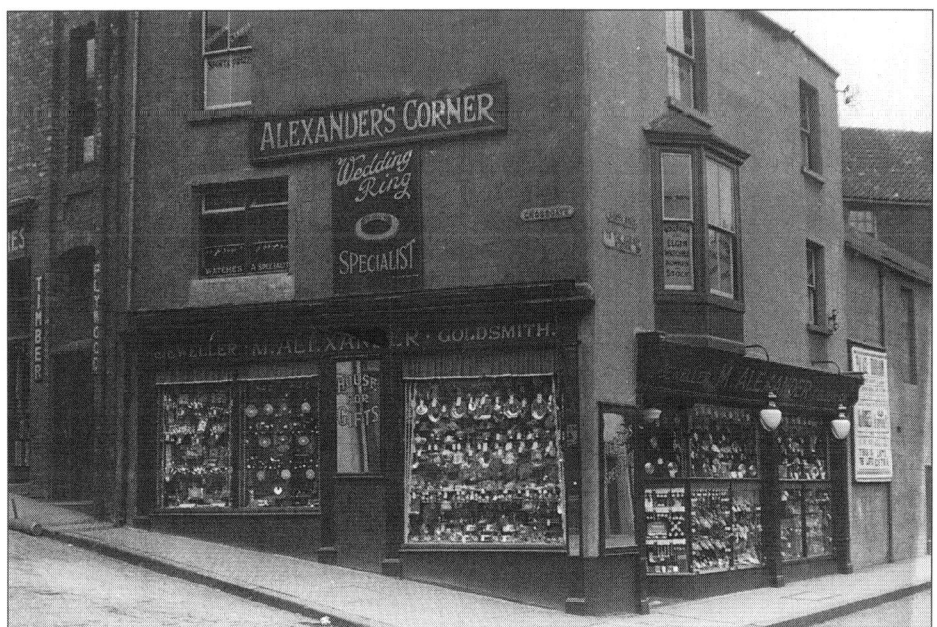

Alexander's Jewellers, 1 North Road, April 1935. In 1902 Mr M. Alexander began business in South Shields and later went on to open several branches in the north. The Durham branch opened in May 1926. The site is now occupied by the Halifax Building Society. The poster on the right is advertising the Palace Cinema in Walkergate.

One of Matthew Fowler's removal wagons from New Elvet, seen at Crossgate Peth, April 1935. This business, including that of Auctioneer and Estate Agent, was established in March 1906, when a small office in Durham Market Place was rented at the premises of Messrs Swanson. He later took over part of the property of Joseph Johnson's Brewery, New Elvet. The railings on the right protect the slope of Crossgate Peth.

A group of schoolboys from Sherburn Village visiting the printing works of the *Durham County Advertiser*, 45 Saddler Street, June 1935.

The opening of Durham County Hospital bazaar in Durham Indoor Market. Amongst the guests on the platform are Lady Surtees, Dean Alington, Lady Londonderry and the Bishop of Jarrow, Dr J.G. Gordon, 22 October 1935.

'We will remember them', a picture taken on Remembrance Day at Brancepeth Village smithy, showing the horseshoe archway. The blacksmith, Robert Tindale, had succeeded his father in the business, 11 November 1935. The young boy is his son, Geoffrey.

The Bridge Hotel, North Road, near to total destruction after the fire which occurred shortly after 3.30am in the bar, 27 December 1935. The fire was so intense that nearby homes had to be evacuated; fortunately no one was injured. The landlord was Mr Alexander Burr. The fire was attended by the City Brigade and the Houghton-Le-Spring Collieries Fire & Rescue Brigade.

An interior view of Earl brothers' confectioners' shop, 68 Saddler Street, October 1935. People queued for their famous meat pies. The shop was next to Masons the Chemist (now Waterstone's).

The Roman Catholic Gala procession leaving Palace Green with the Children of Mary, 1 August 1935. High Mass had been sung earlier in the day in the picturesque grounds of Springwell Hall, North End, which later became St Leonard's Roman Catholic School.

27 July 1935 - Miners' Gala

Gala speakers
Sir Stafford Cripps MP; Mr Hannen Swaffer; the Rt Hon Herbert Morrison MP and Mr George Lansbury MP.

Cathedral service
Preacher: The Revd Spencer Wade, Rector of Wark-on-Tyne, Newcastle.

Brancepeth Colliery Band, bandmaster J.B. Wright.
Burnhope Colliery Band, bandmaster J. Johnson.
Brandon Colliery Band, bandmaster J. Oliver.

Mayor: Councillor Thomas Plummer.

Historical Notes
25 January
Mr Edward Moore elected agent for the Durham Miners' Association.

16 June
Death of Peter Lee (1864-1935), general secretary of the DMA and chairman of the first Labour-controlled County Council.

8 October
Clement Attlee is elected to succeed George Lansbury as Labour leader.

14 November
General Election. Labour Party in Durham County won all County Divisional seats and also the borough of South Shields.

18 November
Explosion at Dean and Chapter Colliery, one life lost (A. Blood).

North Hetton Colliery, Low Moorsley, ceased production.

Blackhall banner, draped in black, approaches The Racecourse, 1935. The photograph was taken by James Jarché, the accompanying caption reading: 'Revolution looks placid in a bowler hat.'

Spectators in deep thought as they listen to Hannen Swaffer. The attendance this year was estimated between at 150,000 and 200,000.

Mr Hannen Swaffer, the flamboyant journalist. He wrote a report of the Gala for the *Daily Herald*. After the Gala he presented an album of photographs of the day to each of the four speakers. These were taken by James Jarché, one of the leading news photographers of the time.

Sir Stafford Cripps (1889-1952) on the speakers' platform, pausing during his speech. He called upon the miners not to lose sight of their great goal when the workers would control the country, their own lives and their safety. "Until that time is reached," he said, "we must go on fighting ruthlessly against exploitation by capitalism." Largely self-educated, he had helped to found the London Labour Party.

Herbert Morrison (1888-1965), photographed in action on the platform. He was the grandfather of Peter Mandelson, the former MP for Hartlepool and former Northern Ireland Secretary.

Herbert Morrison (left) and Mr Ritson, seated on the speakers' platform taking it all in. Swaffer's caption for this photograph read: "Josh Ritson wonders where he has heard it. Morrison never wonders."

Mr George Lansbury (1859-1940) MP, in full swing. He was a strong supporter of womens' suffrage and defender of conscientious objectors. In 1912 he founded and edited the *Daily Herald*. He was leader of the Labour party (1931-35).

Mr George Lansbury greeting two disabled ex-miners in their pony-driven carts.

Mr George Lansbury accepting a sweet from an admirer.

Spectators in joyful mood on the slopes of The Racecourse. They are all wearing their 'Sunday best'.

Father is left holding the baby while grandmother reads the newspaper.

The balloon man prepares his wares for a busy day, eyed by a couple of prospective customers. Pelaw Wood can be seen in the distance.

Getting into the swing of things. The showground was a long-established popular attraction at the Gala.

The orderly crowds being directed from The Racecourse by a lone policeman, making their way to the Cathedral for the miners' service. The preacher at the service was the Revd Spencer Wade, himself once a pit-putter at West Auckland Colliery.

Homeward-bound banners make their way up Elvet Bridge towards the Market Place. The mass of people can be seen as far back as Old Elvet.

Blackhall banner makes its way home from The Racecourse. It is draped in black to commemorate a death in the colliery during the past year.

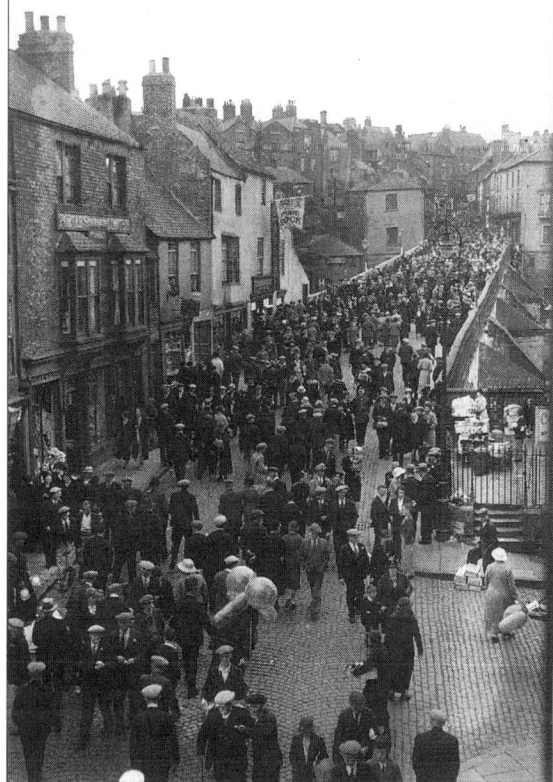

Early afternoon and a quieter scene looking towards Elvet Bridge. On the left is a branch of Porter's, the family grocers, and further to the centre is the 'Rock Shop'.

1936

Red setter puppies, six out of a family of 13 belonging to Mr & Mrs Frederick C. Goodyear of Lowes Barn, Elvet Moor, January 1936. Fred was the son of Alderman Frank W. Goodyear, builder and brickyard owner.

Craftsmen of Durham are seen in the ancient workshops of Durham Cathedral, January 1936. They are Walter Hollis (centre), W.S. Cope (right), and young Thomas Jopling (left), who is standing beside the magnificently-carved door which was dedicated 29 January to the memory of his grandfather, the late W.H. Jopling. The carving of this door, which is the north entrances to St Cuthbert's Shrine was begun by Mr Jopling shortly before his death and was completed by Mr Hollis.

Soldiers from the 8th Battalion Durham Light Infantry, in procession to the cathedral for King George V's memorial service, 28 January 1936. The Dean, Dr C.A. Alington, gave the address to a congregation of about 4,000.

The Northern Counties' Amateur Brass Band Association contest at Durham drew bands from all parts of the county, 1 February 1936. Lumley Colliery band won two trophies. The picture shows an interested crowd listening to one of the bands.

Councillor J. C. Fowler, Deputy Mayor of Durham, presenting medals & bars at the annual social gathering of St Margaret's Church Lad's Brigade, 25 February 1936. On the right is Major H. Cecil Ferens.

A crew from St Mary's College landing at Brown's Boathouse after rowing the course 26 May 1936. They had been taking part in a timed race with Armstrong College, Newcastle. The Armstrong crew won by 19 seconds.

Durham Colleges 'Rag' students, 17 June 1936. They were about to tour the surrounding districts selling the 'Rag' magazine in aid of the Durham County Hospitals. Three days later, the airship Hindenberg passed over the city.

A performance of *The Wraggle-Taggle Gypsies* by Durham Folk Dance Group at Brancepeth Castle's Folk Dancing Festival, June 1936.

Students from St Hild's College, photographed tidying the cathedral churchyard, with young helpers, during the Mothers' Union Festival, 13 July 1936.

An assembly of mothers outside the north door of the cathedral after the Mothers' Union festival service. The Revd Canon O.C. Quick preached the sermon, 13 July 1936.

'Telfer's Boys' Harmonica Band, Framwellgate Moor, July 1936.

A group of excited boys from East Howle School, Ferryhill, playing on the gun in the courtyard of Durham Castle, 11 August 1936. The gun was a trophy from World War One.

A works outing from Holiday's brick works, Sidegate, 19 September 1936. Thomas Holiday, the owner, is pictured on the extreme right, photographed in Durham Market Place prior to departure.

The City Fish & Game Co., 3 New Elvet, October 1936, showing Mr S. Hedley, the fishmonger, arranging the open window display.

Durham Civic Plate, and that of the old Trade Guilds, displayed in the Town Hall, when members of the National Association of Cathedral Old Choristers were visiting Durham, 19 September 1936. Eighty representatives from 16 associations took part.

The wedding of Miss Elizabeth Alington and Lord Dunglas, MP, Durham Cathedral, 3 October 1936. The daughter of Dean Alington, the bride wore a gold-coloured dress. After the ceremony 500 guests attended a reception at the Deanery.

A group of the Jarrow Marchers stop for dinner near Farewell Hall on their way to London, 9 October 1936. About 200 men had set off from Jarrow to hand in a petition against the level of unemployment and also the means-test. While here two medical students from London attended to their blistered feet. Charles Errington, an ex-Northumberland Fusilier cook prepared a tasty pan of broth for the marchers' lunch.

Lady Londonderry, Mayoress of Durham, drawing aside the Union Jack at the formal opening, revealing the name, 'Alington Place', 11 November 1936. These 24 houses, named after Dean Alington, had been erected at Mill Lane, Gilesgate, by the Church Army Housing. They were built for low-wage earners with large families; rents were 7s 1d for a 3-bedroom and 7s 4d for a 4-bedroom.

Mr G. Cummings, gardener for the Dean & Chapter, the occupant of Nursery Cottage, Quarry Heads Lane, Durham, photographed after gales of 70 miles per hour hit Durham, 27 October 1936.

The Bishop of Durham (Dr Hensley Henson) dedicating Alington Place. Left to right, the Revd C.K. Pattison, Revd G.H. Aird, vicar of St Giles's Church, and the Bishop with Lady Londonderry, 11 November 1936. Mr D. McIntyre designed the houses, which were built by Councillor, F.W. Goodyear. The Dean and Chapter contributed £200 towards the cost.

A house party at Wynyard Hall given by Lord and Lady Londonderry, the new Mayor & Mayoress of Durham, November 1936. Left to right, standing: Lord Londonderry, Herr von Ribbentrop, the German Ambassador, Sir Ronald Graham, Mrs Roger Lumley, Mrs Kerr, Mr Roger Lumley, MP for York, Lord Durham, Sir Hedworth Williamson and Lord Castlereagh. Seated: Lady Durham, Frau von Ribbentrop, Lady Londonderry and Lady Castlereagh.

Herr von Ribbentrop and Lord Londonderry, November 1936. von Ribbentrop had been the guest of Lord Londonderry and was later to attend a civic service at Durham Cathedral on the 15th of that month. At the end of the service the British and German National Anthems were played by the cathedral organist, Mr Conrad Eden.

Belmont schoolboy's football team, 1936. Back row: J. Lisgo, J. Clough, Mr Spavin, E. Passmore, J. Mallion, Mr Venner, B. Sutherland and J. Nixon. Middle row: Jos Davies, Bill Garside, E. Dobson, L. Tempest and Jack Coulson. Front row: W. Scott and Reg Martin.

City of Durham Football Club, c.1936. (formed c.1919). It won the North Eastern League Championship 1924-25, and was runner-up (Division Two) for the season 1930-31. Among the internationals produced by this club were G. Camsell, S. Crooks and G. Stevenson. Back row, left to right: F. Footer (chairman), G. King, R. Woolrych (trainer), J. Harrison, N. Swales (captain), J. Blenkinsop, G. Moore and F. Woolrych (secretary). Front row: J. Burns, S. Glidden, R. Littledyke, W. Towers and H. Emery. Sammy Crooks went on to play for Derby County and England. George Camsell made his name with Middlesbrough and England.

Durham St Nicholas FC, 1936. Member of the Ryhope and District Wednesday League, this club was formed in 1929. In the season 1934-35 it reached the final of the City of Durham Medal Competition and in 1935-36 was in the final of the League Challenge Cup. Left to right, back row: G. Grabham (secretary), B. Humphreys (committee), R. Sands, W. Scarr, W. Atkinson, J. Routh, R. Roxborough (captain), G. Scarr and G. Gales (trainer). Front row: G. Dimambro, W. Craig, G. Porter, N. Fleming and R. Peele.

Belmont Red Triangle FC, c.1936, member of the Durham City and District League. In the season 1932-33 it won the Sherburn Aged Miners' Homes Cup and reached the final of the Durham City and District League. Back row, left to right: T. Miller (committee), J. Lee (committee), T. Rowntree (committee), H. Byfield (trainer), H. Robson (committee), H. Barker, J. Laws, T. Bunce, J. Bell, J. Palmer, E. Makepeace (chairman), W. Marley (secretary) and R. Marley (committee). Second row: C. Riley (captain), H. Wilson and T. Cooper. Seated on the ground: T. Unsworth, W. Coffey, T. Sommerbell, C. Thompson and J. Hamilton.

Sacriston Football Club, c.1936. Twice winners of Chester-le-Street Ambulance Cup and Durham Hospital County Cup, also Durham Central League Champions on two occasions. Back row, left to right, back row: J. Embleton, J. Smailes, F. Anson, M. Mordue, N. Crossman, J. Chapman (captain) and C. Shields. Front row: G. White, T. Darwen, R. Drape and O. McGinn.

Bowburn Welfare FC, c.1936, member of the Durham and City District League. It won the Durham Aged Miners' Cup and Durham District Knockout Cup in 1933-34 and 1935-36; also the Sherburn Aged Miners' Cup 1933-34. Back row, left to right: G. Arkwright (committee), J. Fishburn (secretary), W. Atkinson, W. Burbanks (committee), L. Roberts, P. Lovatt, S. Bestford, C. Mitchell (committee), J. Flannagan, S. Mould (committee), S. Heatherington, R. Arkwright (committee) and R. Freeman (committee). Front row: H. Burnett, R. Spence (captain), A. Allison, W. Mitchell, H. Alderson and J. Tipland (trainer).

West Rainton Labour Party FC, c.1936. Back row, left to right: I. Bowater (committee), W. Kelly (committee), R. Groswaite (trainer), M. McIllwraith (committee), R. Vine (committee), J. Vine, E. Bates, T. Teal (committee), W. Dawson, G. Dunning (vice-chairman), W. Fawcett, J. Sheldon (chairman), J. Lawrence, E. Dunning (committee), J. Storey (committee) and E. Griffiths (committee). Front row: G. Perry (secretary), F. Hall, R. Wise, J. Willis (captain), S. Wheatley, W. Perry and T. Kelly.

Brandon (Social) FC, c.1936. Member of the Durham Central League, it was formed in 1931. Its best season was 1934-35 when it won the League, Deerness Aged Miners' Cup & Brandon Nursing Cup. Back row, left to right: D. White (trainer), J. Oliver, A. Birch, A. Clough, W. Dixon, W. Ruddock (captain), and T. Dodds. Front row: J. Joyce, D. Breen, R. Halliday, E. Carter and H. Pickney.

25 July 1936 - Miners' Gala

Gala speakers
Joseph Jones; the Rt Hon Arthur Greenwood MP; Mr C.R. Attlee MP and Mr E. Shinwell MP.

Cathedral service
Preacher: The Rt Revd James Geoffrey Gordon, Bishop of Jarrow.

Brancepeth Colliery Band, bandmaster Mr J.B. Wright.
Burnhope Colliery Band, bandmaster Mr J. Johnson.
Brandon Colliery Band, bandmaster Mr J. Oliver.

Mayor: Councillor W.R.H. Gray.

Historical Notes
This year the miners' hymn tune, *Gresford*, was composed by ex-miner Robert Saint. It was dedicated 'to the memory of all miners who have perished in the mines'.

January.
The DMA appointed a full-time solicitor, Mr R.W. Williams, to take charge of compensation and matters of law.

1 July
Mr Sam Watson elected Agent of the DMA.

11 November
The Jarrow Crusade 'snubbed' by the Prime Minister, Stanley Baldwin, who refused to meet the marchers when they arrived in London.

24 November
Explosion at Thornley Colliery, one life lost (R. Waller).
During this year Bishop Middleham and West Thornley collieries ceased production.

Sacriston officials leading their banner up Silver Street. The portraits are those of Robert Smillie (1857-1946), President of the Miners' Federation of Great Britain (left); and Lord Sankey, Chairman of the Coal Industry Commission – his report brought about a shorter working week and increased wages for all colliery workers.

Mr Clement Attlee MP (1883-1967) addresses the crowd from No. 2 platform. He had been elected to succeed George Lansbury as Labour leader on 8 October 1935. He openly condemned the means test and said the country needs a strong socialist government that would deal with the causes of poverty and sweep away means test legislation and give to the miners a standard of life based on what the country can afford to all its citizens.

Mr Attlee greets a supporter. The three central figures (left to right) are William Whiteley MP, Mr J.R. Leslie MP, and Mr Attlee. One of the speakers was Mr Shinwell, who had defeated Ramsay MacDonald as member for Seaham in 1935, he said the Gala was 'a wonderful demonstration of working-class solidarity'. This was the fifth time he had spoken at the Gala.

Mr Attlee and Mr Whiteley mingle with the crowd. In his speech Attlee had congratulated the Durham Miner on such a remarkable demonstration of loyalty, which he said was an indication of the desire of the workers for a full life and a determination to get it.

The escapologist is tied up by his assistant. A volunteer bandsman double-checks that the chains are secure. They are watched closely by a spellbound audience. The banner is that of West Stanley.

After the speeches and picnic father takes the children off for some fun.

The bandsmen take the ladies for a trip on the river. One of the attractions of the day was the hire of a boat from Brown's boathouse.

1937

The unveiling of the portrait of Dr J.S.G. Pemberton, President of the Council of Durham Colleges, at Durham Castle, 16 February 1937. Left to right: Mr T.C. Dugdale, (the artist), Dr Pemberton, the Marquis of Londonderry (Chancellor of the University), who unveiled the portrait, and the Bishop of Durham (Dr Hensley Henson).

Some of the 100 members of the Durham County Constabulary on the southbound platform at Durham Railway Station, 11 May 1937. They were drafted to London to assist in street duties on Coronation Day (12 May). On the left is Supt. Knaggs of Chester-le-Street. Note that some are wearing their First World War medals.

Graceful young dancers, who were trained by Misses E. & S. McCoull of the Morton House School of Dancing, Tynemouth, photographed after they had enjoyed a happy night at the Town Hall, 12 April 1937.

A delivery boy making his way back into the city from Pimlico at the top of South Street, March 1937.

Dancing pupils of Miss Smith and Miss Marjorie Liddle assembled in the Town Hall for their annual ball, 24 March 1937. They disported themselves in many of the latest dance movements before a large audience.

Robert Dixon of Belmont, working at Holiday & Co Ltd, Manufacturing Chemist, Claypath, April 1937. He was one of two lucky young lads chosen to represent the Belmont Branch of the YMCA at the coronation of King George VI in London.

Newspaper House, 64 Saddler Street (the office of *The Durham County Advertiser*), decorated for the coronation, received first prize for the best-decorated Durham City business premises, 12 May 1937. The building was originally that of the North Eastern Banking Company, and was built in 1898.

The march past after the coronation service in Durham Cathedral, Sunday, 9 May 1937. Various groups of Church Lads' Brigades, Scouts and Guides from the county took part in the procession, as well as a detachment of the 8th Battalion Durham Light Infantry.

The Mayor of Durham, Lord Londonderry, at the saluting base on Palace Green after the coronation service in the cathedral, 9 May 1937. Others in the picture are Colonel W.B. Greenwell, Lady Londonderry, Mr & Mrs W.R.H. Gray (Deputy Mayor & Mayoress) and Alderman F.W. Goodyear.

A garage fire near 'Bunnygarth' The Grove, North End, Durham City, the residence of Mr John McAlmont, 26 May 1937. The city fire brigade tackled it but the garage and the car were totally destroyed. About 30 rare birds from a nearby aviary had to be released for fear of them being killed by the fumes; only two were re-caught.

The entrance of the heralds prior to the crowning of the May Queen, Joan Francis, aged 10, at Bluecoat School, Claypath, 24 May 1937. This festival was started at the school in 1933.

The Mayor & Mayoresss, Lord and Lady Londonderry, with pupils of Bluecoat School at their Empire Day festival, 24 May 1937. Lady Londonderry was photographed amongst the girls who had formed the choir.

A group photo of Durham City golfers at Mount Oswald with their special guests Alfred H. Padgham and the open champion, Henry Cotton, 27 May 1937. They took part in an exhibition match played over 18 holes; Henry Cotton won. The event was organised as part of the club's Jubilee programmes.

The 'Tipster' at the Durham 'Rag' races, 18 June 1937. The *Durham County Advertiser* carried the humorous caption, 'I've got an 'orse! I've got an 'orse! The owner's going to back it. The trainer's going to back it. I want you to back it. It'll romp home at 33-1'.

Bearpark schoolboys' football team, June 1937, winner of the Deerness Valley Schools' League Shield and the Ushaw Moor Aged Miners' Cup. Back row, left to right: Mr Walter Grainger, Eric Joyce, Robert Seed, Leslie Colwell, Joseph Corker, Thomas Minns, Thomas Wilson and Mr Thomas Wilson. Middle row, seated: Dennis Belshaw, George Ruddick, Ronald Thompson (captain), Mr Herbert Chicken (headmaster), Edwin Winn, Lawrence Smith and Mr Aaron Pearson (deputy headmaster). Front row: James Smallwood and Robert Thornton.

The students' representation of the 'Mayor and Corporation' complete with sword, and mace-bearers and bodyguard, at the 'Rag' procession, Palace Green, 18 June 1937.

University policemen, Sergt-Major Gray, ex-DLI, left, and Sergt. William Plunkett on Palace Green, July 1937. The University police are believed to be older than the county force, having been formed around the time that the first students were admitted in 1833.

The visit of the Duke of Kent to the Haig Homes, Sutherland Place, Sherburn Road Estate, 13 July 1937. The Mayor, Lord Londonderry, is seen to the right wearing his chain of office. The street was named after Sir Arthur Munro Sutherland who had contributed substantially towards the cost of the homes, 18 houses were built with a rent of 6s 7d per week. The Haig Homes movement owned 361 houses and flats in 13 centres throughout the country.

The Duke of Kent being greeted by the headmaster of Durham School, the Revd H.K. Luce, 13 July 1937. The Duke was the first member of the royal family to visit the school. During a conversation with the headmaster the Duke asked that his visit might be commemorated by an extra day's holiday. It was understood that the wish was complied with. The school chapel, a memorial to past pupils who were killed in World War One, stands high on the hill.

A physical fitness display at the city cricket ground on The Racecourse at Durham, July 1937. On the far right is the Pineapple Inn, Old Durham Gardens.

The funeral procession of the Deputy Mayor, Councillor W.R.H. Gray MA, JP, approaching the cathedral, 28 July 1937. He died suddenly on the evening of the Miners' Gala while attending dinner with the miners' leaders at the Royal County Hotel. He was the son of the late Mr William Gray JP and was a former pupil of Bede Model School, Gilesgate. On the death of his father he took over the business of University Robemakers & Gentlemen's Outfitters in Saddler Street and also opened a branch in Newcastle.

The deferred coronation tea for old folk from the city. The venue was Durham Indoor Market, 22 July 1937. The Mayor, Lord Londonderry, presented the oldest man and woman with £1 each.

Giant 'puff balls' monsters of the fungus world, which were growing near Kepier, October 1937. Some have been known to grow to such a size that they have been mistaken for sheep from a distance.

Mayor's Day at Durham, 9 November 1937. Lord and Lady Londonderry are photographed, prior to the swearing in of the new mayor. They are seen with members of the bodyguard and, at the rear, Alderman P.J. Waite. The new mayor was William Ewart Bradley.

Durham school children at the Palladium Cinema, Claypath, December 1937. A special Christmas treat had been organised for them by the *Durham County Advertiser* readers. On the right is Alderman T.W. Holiday, owner of the Palladium. The lady on the right is Minnie Clark, wife of Benny, who had the toyshop opposite.

Excited children at the Palladium, December 1937. The boy second from the left is Ronnie Clark. Around 800 children from poor homes in the city were entertained. Packets containing fruit, sweets and a new penny were presented to each child. The Palladium was opened 18 March 1929.

Milkmaids at Durham County Council's Farm, Houghall, December 1937. The photograph was taken as part of a national campaign to promote the benefits of milk as the nation's cheapest food.

24 July 1937 - Miners' Gala

Gala speakers
The Rt Hon H. Morrison MP; Professor H. Laski; Sir Stafford Cripps MP (and Lady Cripps) and Mr Ebby Edwards.

Cathedral service
Preacher: The Revd R.W. Stannard, Bishop Wearmouth, Sunderland.

Brancepeth Colliery Band, bandmaster Mr J.B. Wright.
Burnhope Colliery Band, bandmaster Mr J. Johnson.
Brandon Colliery Band, bandmaster Mr J. Oliver.

Mayor: Lord Londonderry.

Historical Notes
15 May
One hour reduction from 49 hours per week to 48 hours.

28 May
Neville Chamberlain succeeds Stanley Baldwin as Prime Minister.

19 October
Explosion at Hamsterley Colliery, one life lost.

21 December
Explosion at Murton Colliery, four lives lost (John McKillup, Richard Spry, John Simmons and Thomas Monarch). There were 10,336 horses and ponies working in the Durham Coalfield this year.

Mr J.R. Leslie MP, Dr Hugh Dalton MP and Mr W. Whiteley MP (with pipe) photographed beside the platform.

Sir Stafford Cripps MP and Lady Cripps walking among the crowd on The Racecourse. He had spoken on the platform for one hour, warning the miners that collaboration with capitalists might wreck Labour's future.

Crowds rest on the slopes of The Racecourse. The attendance this year was around 200,000. Note, top left, the caravans belonging to the showmen.

'All in together!' Bandsmen take a hand in the fun.

The crèche on The Racecourse, a welcome addition for the miners' wives. This was the first time it had been introduced to the Gala. The idea for this was the brainchild of Mrs Hesther Alington, wife of the Dean. She and her friends made themselves responsible for the organisation, which was later taken over by the Mothers' Union.

Left in charge while mother and father listen to the speakers

The family settle down to eat their picnic lunch, making good use of the big bass drum.

'I scream, you scream, we all scream for ice-cream' – this was the caption of the original photograph. Notice the smart attire and the fashionable headgear.

1938

Staff outside the United Shoe Shop, Elvet Bridge, c.1938, showing Vince Edwards, in the white apron, and, second from the left, Wilf Mollon. The shop was to the left of Bramwell the Jeweller. It later moved to Saddler Street.

An unusual view from the inside of T. & C. Heslops' butcher's shop, 85 New Elvet, now Prontaprint, February 1938. W.J. Heslop started the business in May 1895 at 4 New Elvet. In about 1937 it became a limited company when Mr R. Morton came in as a partner with the founder's two sons.

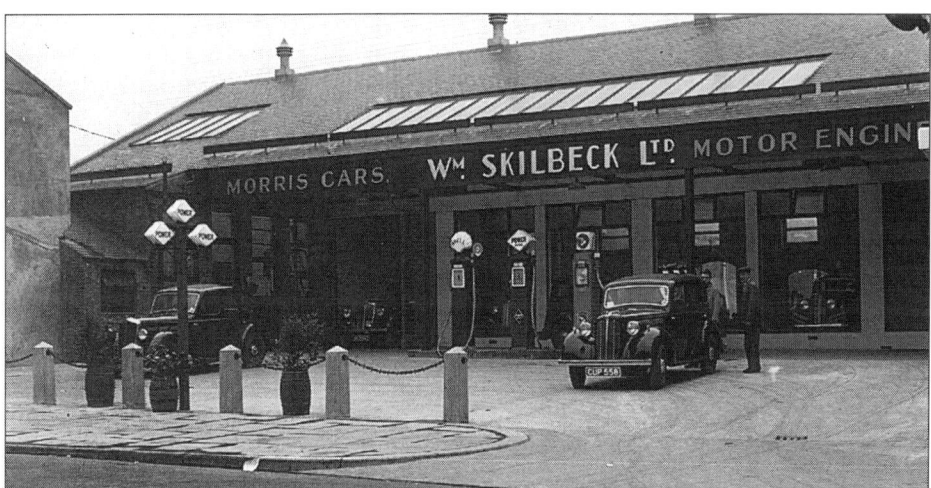

Skilbeck's Garage, Langley Moor, March 1938. The firm was established at Annfield Plain in 1913. Councillor R. Bone JP, Chairman of Brandon & Byshottles Urban District Council, officially opened the garage 2 March 1938.

Cheerful children from Bluecoat School, Claypath receive sand-shoes for their sports activities, as part of the government's national fitness campaign, February 1938.

Mrs C. Bowers of Greenfield Terrace, Sacriston, with her dog Jack. She was believed to be the only woman Caller (knocker-upper) in the mining districts of England, February 1938. Every morning at one o'clock she would leave her warm bed to call the miners up to go to work on the fore-shift. She first started the job as a wartime occupation during World War One.

Mr Elijah Burnside, watch and gramophone repairer, of Brandon, who was blind from birth, March 1938. In his spare time he enjoyed entertaining folk with the playing of some of his several musical instruments.

A 'Keep Fit' class of enthusiasts from the Durham City Girls' Club going through their exercises inside the Drill Hall at the bottom of Gilesgate Bank, 19 February 1938. Front left is Annie Shea.

Playtime at St Godric's Roman Catholic School, Castle Chare, March 1938. The street in the background is Co-operative Terrace, which was demolished when the new road was built linking the Millburngate Bridge to North Road roundabout.

An unusual view of the window-cleaner, showing off some of his acrobatic skill at the *Durham County Advertiser* office, 64 Saddler Street, March 1938.

The opening of the Silver Link footbridge, which connects Gilesgate with Pelaw Wood, 12 April 1938. Alderman J.T.E. Dickenson, on the left, opened the bridge in the presence of the Mayor, Councillor W.E. Bradley. It was designed by the City Engineer, Mr J.W. Green, based on a larger one which crossed the Victoria Falls on the Zambezi River. The Cleveland Bridge Company of Darlington constructed it.

Durham Cathedral Choir, April 1938, photographed in the chancel with the Neville Screen and the Rose Window in the background.

President of the Hospital, Lord Londonderry, laying the foundation stone for the £60.000 extension to the Durham County Hospital, North Road, 7 May 1938. He had just recovered from a fractured collar-bone, suffered during a golfing holiday with the Prime Minister in Scotland.

Mr H.S. Harrison, Chairman of the Durham County Hospital Management Committee, explained the necessity for the extensions of the work at the hospital, 7 May 1938. The firm of Cordingley & McIntyre designed the extension and the builders were George Gradon & Son, North Road.

The newly-opened Neville Dene Hotel (now a Sainsbury's Local), Crossgate Moor, 7 May 1938. It was opened by the Mayor, Councillor W.E. Bradley, and was built by Thomas Clements & Sons Ltd. of Newcastle. The name of the hotel was chosen through a competition, although it was later renamed after the old Pot & Glass which stood at the bottom of Tollhouse Road.

The Student 'Rag', June 1938. The City Corporation, like many other businesses, loaned its wagons and drivers for the annual charity event.

The retaining wall for the footpath near South Street Mill, being built by the Dean & Chapter and Durham City Council, June 1938. On the far left is the spire of St Nicholas's Church in the Market Place.

The funeral of the Bishop of Jarrow, Dr James Geoffrey Gordon, August 1938. The body had lain overnight in the Chapel of the Nine Altars, He was buried near to the South African War Memorial in the cathedral churchyard. He had been appointed in 1932.

Girls from Mackay's Carpet Factory, Walkergate, brushing and finishing off carpets, October 1938. The old factory site is now part of Millennium Place, Claypath.

Rebecca Birch, Herbalist, 25 Market Place, a member of the National Association of Medical Herbalists, October 1938. Health foods were almost unknown in the Durham district before she began business. She served her apprenticeship with her father, John Birch, who had been a qualified Medical Herbalist for 54 years. She passed the final Examination of the College of Botanical Medicine in 1932.

Bower Bank, the name of the lane and area behind St Giles's Church, Gilesgate, October 1938. This name, which is now almost forgotten, is mentioned in St Giles's tithe records in 1655.

Doggart's shop in the Market Place (now Boots Chemists), October 1938. The Durham City shop was opened in 1923. The firm had started with one shop in Bishop Auckland in 1895. By the 1930s it had grown to be one of the most progressive in the north of England.

Gloria Dawn as Cinders, aged 16, December 1938. A pupil of the Durham County Girls' School. Her real name was Gloria Turnbull and she lived in Albert Street, Durham City. She was photographed prior to her debut at a theatre in Darlington.

Mrs Hodgson, her daughter, Eliza and son, John, of New Brancepeth, had a remarkable escape when their car was caught by a skidding omnibus at the entrance to Cross Street (now part of Hawthorn Terrace), next to the Colpitts public house, 19 December 1938.

23 July 1938 - Miners' Gala

Gala speakers
George Lansbury MP; Mr C.R. Attlee MP; the Rt Hon A. Greenwood MP; Mr Joseph Jones; also visitors Mr Alexei Nikolenko, President of the Don-bas miners, USSR, and Dr Camps, a lady from Spain.

Cathedral service
Preacher: The Very Revd C.A. Alington, Dean of Durham.

Brancepeth Colliery Band, bandmaster Mr J.B. Wright.
Burnhope Colliery Band, bandmaster Mr J. Johnson.
Brandon Colliery Band, bandmaster Mr J. Oliver.

Mayor: Councillor W.E. Bradley.

Historical Notes
16 March
Explosion at Ravensworth Colliery, one life lost.

14 April
Miners' holidays-with-pay agreement to take effect from August.

June
Burnhope Colliery introduced a scheme prohibiting boys under the age of 16 from working underground.

October
A fund was launched by the DMA in support of oppressed Czechoslovakian workers.

November
The DMA Executive Committee forwarded resolutions to the Labour Party, Foreign Secretary and the Prime Minister condemning the brutal and inhuman treatment meted out by the Nazi Government to the men, women and children of the Jewish race.

Sword dancers outside the Waterloo Hotel, Old Elvet. The building on the left was the County Court offices.

Crowds gather on The Racecourse. The allotments laid out on the other side of the river were worked by the lady students of St Hild's College. A small poster in the centre reads: 'Nuts & Raisins 1d a Bag'.

A trader sells his wares from a cart. The banners (left to right) are those of Sherburn Hill, Sherburn House and Craghead.

Mr Alexei Nikolenko, President of the Don-bas miners (the largest mining district in Russia) talking to Mr Clement Attlee MP on the speakers' platform. The president's speech was relayed to the crowd by an interpreter. He said one of the most important questions was the struggle against Fascism. Germany, Italy and Japan were preparing more terrors against democratic countries. "War may break out at any moment," he said, "and we must spare no strength in trying to avert it through the solidarity of the working class."

A group of miners listening carefully to George Lansbury. In his speech he told the crowd that he wished very much that the President of the French Republic and King George could have stood on the same balcony as "we ourselves and seen the march, representing the real strength and vitality of the Durham Miners".

The Russian miners' leader, Alexei Nikolenko (left) with Mr William Lawther MP. The latter, from Chopwell, had become chairman of the British National Committee of the Friends of Soviet Russia.

The Rt Hon Arthur Greenwood (1880-1954) MP, seated on the slopes of The Racecourse, engages in conversation with a retired miner. Greenwood Aged Miners' Homes, Thornley, were named after him (see Thornley Banner).

A solemn crowd with hats removed listens to the band playing the hymn tune *Gresford* before the speeches begin. This tune was named after the Welsh mining disaster (22 September 1934) when 264 died.

An early afternoon scene on the river bank. Opposite is seen the new concrete retaining wall for Pelaw Wood footpath. In the distance is the old bandstand.

'Stick 'em where you like', was the original caption. Bandsmen try their luck with darts at one of the side-shows. Boxes of chocolates under the dartboards await the lucky contestants.

'Back to back' gave comfort and support to both parties at snack hour.

East Hetton (Kelloe) banner, Kelloe, preparing to leave The Racecourse. On it is the portrait of A.J. Cook with the motto: 'Faithful unto death'. Mr Cook (1883-1931) was a Welsh miner who became secretary of the Miners' Federation of Great Britain.

Crookhall banner on the move towards Old Elvet.

A banner making its way home along Old Elvet, draped in black.

1939

The King and Queen arrived by the Royal train at Durham Railway Station, where Lord and Lady Londonderry, Lord Lieutenant of the County, received them, 23 February 1939. The main purpose of the visit was to enable Their Majesties to see and inspect the houses that had been erected in recent years on the Sherburn Road Estate.

A royal visit to Durham by King George VI and Queen Elizabeth, 23 February 1939. About 3,000 school-children assembled in the Market Place to sing the national anthem, under the conductorship of Mr Oliver May of Durham Cathedral Choir.

The King and Queen visiting houses on the new council estate on Sherburn Road, 23 February 1939. They are seen leaving the home of Mr and Mrs William Wright of 24 Cuthbert Avenue. Both the King and Queen showed keen interest and Her Majesty was particularly impressed with the internal arrangements. The new Pelaw View Community Centre now occupies the site.

The royal couple are seen prior to visiting the home of Mr and Mrs Thomas Albrighton, 22 Fir Avenue, 23 February 1939. The new estate housed about 3,600 people who were formerly resident in dismal and dilapidated property in the heart of the city, Millburngate and Framwellgate.

The Bishop of Hexham & Newcastle, Monsignor J.M. McCormack, photographed after the blessing of the new Roman Catholic Church Hall (now St Joseph's School, Mill Lane) at Gilesgate Moor April 1939.

The Mayor, Councillor Wilf Edge, and Father W.I. Meagher, with members of the Roman Catholic community outside St Joseph's new church hall, April 1939.

Some of the burnt-out cars that were destroyed at the newly-built garage of J. McIntyre & Son, New Elvet, May 1939. The damage was estimated at £3,000. McIntyre's Coachworks were founded in 1896 at Elvet Waterside.

A lorry belonging to S. Snowdon Ltd with its load of fish which had crashed into a telegraph pole near Farewell Hall on the Great North Road, May 1939. What looks like scratches on the photograph are in fact wires from the nearby telegraph pole, which was hit.

A croquet tournament on Palace Green to raise funds for the student 'Rag'. Canon E.F. Braley of Bede College is seen making a shot watched by Mr J.F. Duff, Warden of Durham Colleges, June 1939.

Students in fancy dress for the 'Rag', one of whom is impersonating Adolf Hitler, June 1939. Three months later war was declared on Germany.

Blind couple, Mr J.W. Vest of Hatfield View, New Elvet, and Miss Annie Morrison of Burnhope photographed after they were married at the Registry Office in Claypath, 10 August 1939.

Children from St Leonard's Roman Catholic School, North End, receiving instructions from Mr G.B. Philipson in the fitting of gas masks, August 1939.

Land Army girls seen feeding pigs during their training at the School of Agriculture, Houghall, September 1939. The girls were there for a four-week course to learn the practical & theoretical sides of farming, so as to qualify for membership in the Women's Land Army.

An Observer Corps crew from the city, September 1939. Names on the reverse are: G. Trotter, J.W. Lambert, T.S. Ritson, C. Maude, M. Mellon, F. Dodds, J.R. Gilderoy, T.H. Mole, N. Carpenter and D.E. Webster.

Training at Belmont Park Racecourse, October 1939. A private company had been formed to promote race meetings at Belmont. The site was chosen because the track had been partly laid already. The area is now part of Cheveley Park housing estate.

Harvest Festival at St Nicholas's Church, Market Place, 8 October 1939. The Revd F.H. Pickering is seen on the right conducting the service.

The Rainton Handicap winner, Belle Toi crosses the line at Belmont Park Racecourse, 6 November 1939.

A procession of men and women who were manning the ARP posts around the city attending a cathedral service, accompanied by the new Mayor, Councillor S. Kipling, 12 November 1939. Preparations for the setting up of Air Raid Precautions posts were started at Durham in June 1938.

An Air Raid Precautions Wardens' exercise, December 1939. Wardens are seen treating 'casualties' in the northern part of the city. The mock casualties were volunteers from the 5th Durham Scouts.

Durham City Observer Corps Headquarters, December 1939. Observer Captain E.G. Jones, MBE, MA, the controller of No. 30 group is seen in the background. The man holding the telephone is Mr Donald Webster, Vice Principal of Bede College.

22 July 1939 - Miners' Gala

Gala speakers
Sir Stafford Cripps MP; Mr Aneurin Bevan MP; Mr Ebby Edwards and the Rt Hon Herbert Morrison MP.

Cathedral service
Preacher: The Very Revd Harry William Blackburn, Dean of Bristol.

Blackhall Colliery Band, bandmaster Mr W. Dawson.
Brandon Colliery Band, bandmaster Mr J. Oliver.
Craghead Colliery Band, bandmaster Mr J. Smith.

Mayor: Councillor W.F. Edge.

Historical Notes
27 April
Conscription begins.

15 May
The Bishop of Durham, Dr A.T.P. Williams, descended the pit shaft of Eppleton Colliery on a three-hour tour of the working underground and on the surface.

3 September.
War with Germany declared.

9 November
Air-raid precautions for collieries introduced.

Mr Ben Wright, aged 75, of Brancepeth, the oldest bandmaster in the county, seen conducting the massed bands in the playing of the miners' hymn tune *Gresford*.

The massed bands playing *Gresford* behind the speakers' platform. The speakers and guests are facing the audience.

Relaxing on the slopes of The Racecourse. Aneurin Bevan MP told the crowds that 'never in history had the working classes of this country exerted less influence in the conduct of public affairs' and 'one result was that thousands were earning less than £2 a week'.

Having a ride on the dodgems. Sir Stafford Cripps had spoken earlier in the day of how the interests of the common people were in danger, due to the present Government. He criticised it for the failure to provide deep bomb-proof shelters for the civilian population; also the failure to store large quantities of food. *Photograph by D.E. Webster of Bede College.*

Blackhall banner showing the portraits of A.J. Cook, Peter Lee and Keir Hardie. The great height of the door easily allows the raised banner to enter. Scenes such as this would have been familiar in medieval times when the craftsmen of the city paraded their banners through the town on Corpus Christi Day in June.

Brandon Colliery banner heads towards the great door of the Cathedral for the miners' service. The preacher was the Dean of Bristol, the Very Revd H.W. Blackburn, who said that it was the most moving service he had ever attended. "To see all those miners, their wives and families, crowded into the cathedral was a scene I shall never forget."

Blackhall Band, conducted by Mr W. Dawson, leaving the cathedral playing Schubert's *Unfinished Symphony*.

Blackhall banner after the service, led by their vicar.

Craghead banner, showing David and Goliath, with the motto: 'He that would be free must strike the first blow.' The band, conducted by Mr J. Smith, had taken part in the playing of voluntaries during the service.

Brandon Colliery banner, bearing a portrait of Thomas Carr and a picture of the west end of the cathedral. The latter had painted over a portrait of Ramsay MacDonald after the miners lost faith in him.

The congregation makes its way towards Palace Green. Note (top) the hat-bearer carrying the head-gear of the bandsmen and the men holding the lodge banner.

The morning after on the fairground, photographed by Mr D.E. Webster.

1940

The 'Dee Cee' Works (toffee factory) of Adams (Durham) Ltd., New Elvet, seen during the fire which almost destroyed the site. Durham City Fire brigade brought the fire under control after a 3-hour effort, 3 April 1940.

Durham's new ice-rink, April 1940. Miss Iris Howles from Manchester who was 3rd in the British pairs championship in 1937 and 1938. She is photographed with Mr Adolf Schima of Manchester (right) a bronze, silver and gold medallist, and Mr 'Icey' Smith, owner of the rink. Mr Schima had been appointed as a coach at the rink, lessons being 4s for 40 minutes. (Note the open top.)

A group of ladies assembled in the Prior's Hall of Durham Deanery, working on behalf of the Central Hospitals Supply Service Committee, June 1940. The Hon. Mrs Alington (organiser) is on the extreme left.

Durham Girl Guides and members of girls' clubs who had successfully collected aluminium for the war effort, July 1940. They are seen near Fleming & Neil, ironmongers, Claypath. The old Police Box can be seen in the distance. Dorothy Colman, photographed third from the left, has an extra piece of material added to lengthen her uniform. This was due to the shortage of cloth.

A practice fire call at Durham which was issued by Supt. J.R. Ellwood (in uniform) brought a quick response from his team, photographed near The Sands, August 1940. The building in the background belongs to the sewage works on the opposite side of the river.

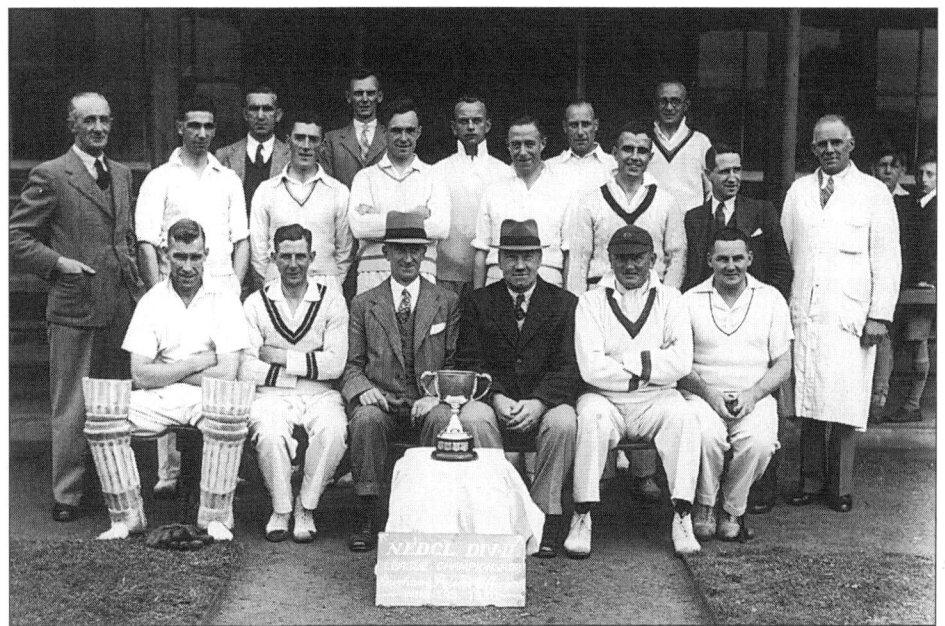

Durham Prison Officers' cricket team which had won the championship of the Second Division of the North East Durham Cricket League, August 1940. Out of 18 matches played, 17 were won and one was drawn. In the centre of the picture is Governor W. Foster and on his left is Chief Officer C. Desbrow.

The Mayor, Councillor Kipling, receiving £6 10s from Vera Tomlinson, Florence Hudson, Elizabeth Chapman and Doreen Chicken, October 1940. This was money they had raised for the Ambulance Fund.

'Bringing in the Sheaves': a member of the Land Army gathering the harvest at Houghall Demonstration Farm, August 1940. The girls were working under the direction of Mr J. Wilson of Houghall Farm.

A window display in North Road organised by the Durham County Allotment Holders' Association, encouraging the citizens of Durham in the 'Dig for Victory' Campaign, October 1940. Mr C. Edmundson of Crook is seen on the right; on the left is Mr L. Buss from Houghall School of Agriculture. People were encouraged to grow onions as, prior to the outbreak of war, most of our onions were imported.

Boys and girls from Bluecoat School, Claypath, photographed after the presentation of junior First Aid certificates, December 1940. Mr H.L. Holliday (right) trained the children and the success rate was 100

Jean Reed skating at Durham Ice Rink, c.1940. Note the open top.

1941

Five Durham girls, Marion Richardson, Marjorie Summerbell, Ann Crofton, Margaret Hall and Maureen Garbutt are seen presenting a cheque for £3 10s to the Mayor Councillor J.F.J. Smith in aid of the Spitfire Fund, Durham Ice Rink, January 1941. The money had been raised by a concert and collection.

The army salvage unit photographed at a munitions dump near Durham, January 1941. Unexploded German bombs, which had been emptied, were cut up for scrap by the oxy-acetylene flame and then sent to the steel furnaces to make bombs and returned back to Germany.

Rabbi Steinberg congratulating the bride and groom at the Jewish Synagogue, Laburnum Avenue, Durham City, 12 February 1941. The groom, Harold Steinberg, on the right, was the son of Mr and Mrs D. Steinberg of Gateshead, and the bride was Mrs Etta Robinson, the youngest daughter of Mrs and the late Mr M. Robinson of 38 Hawthorn Terrace, Durham City (parents of Gerry Steinberg MP). On the left are Mr and Mrs J. Garbutt (sister and brother-in-law of the bride) who themselves had been married 18 years previously in the same synagogue. The bride's niece on the far right is Miss Cynthia Garbutt, the bridesmaid. Rabbi A.C. Steinberg, brother of the bridegroom, came from Manchester to officiate at the ceremony.

Alderman William Smith, chairman of the City Education Committee, lends a hand in the serving of hot school meals at Bluecoat School, Claypath, 18 February 1941. The occasion was the opening of the city's first school canteen which was under the supervision of Miss D. Holliday, domestic science teacher. The menu consisted of vegetable soup followed by jam roll and custard.

Members of Bearpark Women's Institute, present a pageant 'The Masque of the Empire', 18 February 1941. It was produced by Miss A. Grainger, with all proceeds going to the Durham County Hospital.

Miss Cecilia College, 'Queen of the Ice', centre right, Britain's World Champion Amateur Figure Skater, at Durham Ice Rink, 19 March 1941. She is surrounded by her admirers, among whom is the Mayor, Councillor J.F.J. Smith. She had travelled from her home in the West End of London to take part in the first anniversary ice carnival.

Voluntary Services, representing the County of Durham, parade to evensong at Durham Cathedral, 15 June 1941. Many of the Nursing Division and Ambulance Men and Women were from the colliery areas.

The Deputy Mayor, Councillor S. Kipling, among a group of Boy Scouts in the 5th Durham's den under Durham Indoor Market, April 1941. The occasion was the presentation of 25 junior St John's Ambulance badges and certificates following tests.

Sherburn Hill Auxiliary Fire Service (AFS) photographed on the occasion of the presentation of badges and certificates, 19 July 1941. This event took place in the Seven Stars Inn, Sherburn Hill.

Durham's new streamlined fire engine on display for the first time in Durham Market Place, 27 August 1941. On the left are Councillor Wilf Edge and the Deputy Mayor, Councillor S. Kipling, and Mr J. Willis, the chief officer who designed the engine. The fireman second from the right is Mr H. Young.

An Assistance Board Mobile Unit (for the purpose of alleviating distress arising from enemy action) was shown to the citizens for the first time, 11 October 1941. The Mayor, Councillor J.F.J. Smith, welcomed Mr R. D. Brightman, area officer of the unit.

1942

Members of the Air Training Corps (ATC), during 'Warship Week', 1 February 1942. It was hoped that the target of £210.000 would be raised for the city and rural districts to be able to qualify for the 'adoption' of HMS *Witherington D76*, which was on escort duty in the North Atlantic.

Members of the Auxiliary Territorial Service (ATS), later replaced by the Women's Royal Army Corps (WRAC.), marching over Elvet Bridge when they were taking part in 'Warship Week', 1 February 1942. The parade had started in Waddington Street and travelled through the Market Place where Lord Londonderry, Lord Lieutenant of the County, took the salute. It finally ended in Old Elvet.

Two mobile canteens, which were handed over to the North Regional Fire Service by the British Legion of the County of Durham, 30 May 1942. They had been purchased by voluntary subscription from men and women of the Legion. Mr J.J. Lawson MP received them on behalf of Sir Arthur Lambert, Regional Commissioner, to be used by the National Fire Service No.1 Northern Region. The Mayor was Councillor H.L. Gradon.

Soldiers from the 8th Battalion Durham Light Infantry (Home Guard) c.1942 outside Gilesgate Goods Station, c.1939. The building, Durham's first passenger station, opened in June 1844. In more recent times it was Archibald's DIY store. Now an eating establishment and a Travel Lodge.

1946

The Mayor, Councillor J.L. Robson, and other dignitaries, watching the Victory Parade, outside Shire Hall, Old Elvet, 8 June 1946. Captain R.W. Annand, VC, DL is at the rear of the group.

The City Corporation gave a party to 500 old people as part of the Victory Celebrations, 27 June 1946. The Mayor, Councillor J.L. Robson, seen on the right, welcomed them all. Tea was followed by an entertainment in the Town Hall.

A party of 30 Chinese seamen from the crew of SS *Goldmouth* came to see the cathedral and ancient city, 19 July 1946. The Revd J.R. Kay, Minister of the Congregational Church at Durham, and the Revd J. Patton, Regional Chaplain of the British Sailors' Society, North Shields, escorted them.

The Workers' Educational Association students based at Hatfield College, July 1946. Mr B.W. Abrahart is seen outlining the day's programme while assembled on the steps in the castle courtyard. This was the first school held since before the war. It was organised by Durham University Board of Extra-Mural Studies in connection with the WEA.

Miss Hilda Sides, a distinguished London artist, with some of her watercolours of the city beauty spots, August 1946. Photographed in the ballroom of the Dunelm Hotel, Old Elvet.

Honorary Graduates honoured at Hatfield College Centenary, August 1946. Left to right: Mr John Moor, Henry Smith School, West Hartlepool (DCL); Dr C.E. Whiting former Vice-Principal of St Chad's College (D. Litt); and Dr K.C. Dunham, a member of the Geological Survey, London (DSc), who was knighted in 1972.

A cheerful Matthew Ranson of Front Street, Pity Me, riding his AA patrol motorcycle and sidecar through Pity Me, 8 September 1946. The photograph was taken after his guest appearance on the BBC Radio programme, *Country Magazine*

Mr W. Tilley, centre, showing German prisoners-of-war round Durham Cathedral, 27 October 1946. They were attending the harvest festival service, which had been arranged by Lieut. Col G.K. Stobart, Officer Commanding the 93rd POW Camp at Harperley. Part of the camp still survives, hidden among fir trees on the road from Crook to Weardale. Some of the men in the photograph were U-boat crew-members.

Mr Jack Winter, an ex-miner, aged 86, October 1946. A resident of the Almshouses, Owengate, looking out of his window towards the spot where he declared he saw a ghostly figure at 1pm on the 12 October. The ghost is said to be that of a University Don who had committed suicide by throwing himself down the black staircase in the castle.

The Princess Royal with Matron Miss Lee, Lord Londonderry and the Mayor Councillor F. Foster, 21 November 1946. The occasion was the opening of the children's ward, Durham County Hospital, which was named after the former Matron, Miss Margaret Whitlock.

Members of Durham Colleges Dramatic Society, wearing 17th-century dress for the period play *Love for Love* by William Congreve, photographed passing through the Watergate at the end of the South Bailey, December 1946.

Corporal Henry H. Wills of 54 Laurel Avenue, Durham, photographed with his mother and daughter, Margaret, outside Buckingham Palace after being presented with the Distinguished Conduct Medal, December 1946. The DCM was awarded for his bravery in Albania, in 1944, while serving with the Royal Corps of Signals; he was later transferred to the Commandos.

Boys and girls admiring the toys which German prisoners-of-war had made to be presented to the cathedral for needy Durham children, December 1946. Note the diamond patches on the prisoners' clothing.

Here and overleaf: The Dean and Mrs Alington among the German prisoners who had brought the welcome gifts to be placed under the Christmas tree, December 1946. The Dean had lost a son in the war, Capt. Patrick Alington of the 6th Grenadier Guards.

20 July 1946 - Miners' Gala

Gala speakers
The Rt Hon Clement Attlee MP, Prime Minister; the Rt Hon Aneurin Bevan MP, Minister of Health; the Rt Hon Hugh Dalton MP, Chancellor of the Exchequer and Mr Ebby Edwards, Secretary of the NUM.

Cathedral service
Preacher: The Revd J. McManners, Vicar of Ferryhill.

Brancepeth Colliery Band, bandmaster Mr J.B. Wright.
Dean & Chapter Colliery Band, bandmaster Mr W. Graham.
Craghead Colliery Band, bandmaster Mr J. Smith.

Mayor: Councillor J.L. Robson.

Historical Notes
April.
Re-opening of Conishead Priory Convalescent Home, Ulverston, Lancashire.

20 July
First post-war Annual Miners' Gala held.

29 July
Explosion at Addison Colliery; two lives lost (N. Priestey and B. Sweeney)

23 December
Explosion at Ramshaw Colliery, two lives lost (W.A. Hodgson and C. Firby).

There was a shortage of beer at the Gala this year due to strict Government controls by the Ministry of Food.

This year Auckland Park Colliery, Bishop Auckland, ceased production.

The Durham County Brass Band League Championship was won by Hetton Silver Band.

The first post-war Gala seen from Pelaw Wood. Brandon Colliery used this photograph to create its new banner in 1949. *Photograph by Charles Hodgson.*

Lambton Colliery banner showing, on the reverse side, Christ walking on the sea, with the motto: 'Oh thou of little faith wherefore didst thou doubt?' The attendance was estimated at around 200,000.

Cornsay banner, followed by that of Waterhouses, enters The Racecourse.

The Prime Minister, the Rt Hon Clement Attlee, speaking from No. 2 platform. Note the BBC microphone. He said: "I think there is no community in Great Britain more understanding than the men and women of the mining community in Durham. Durham County has not only sent a splendid team of MPs to Westminster but a number of them, hold high rank in the Government."

The audience listen to the Prime Minister. The two tents are those of (left) the ambulance team, and (right) lost children. The *Northern Echo* reported: 'The 62nd Durham Miners Gala will be long remembered, not least because of the well-ordered manner of the great crowd and the fact that for the first time in its history the Prime Minister and four other Ministers of the Crown were present.'

The comedian entertaining the young folk under a banner carrying the motto: 'We seek Knowledge that we may wield power.'

A family band consisting of two piano accordions and a drum-kit strike up a tune for afternoon dancing.

Homeward bound (4.10pm by Bramwell's clock). The great crowd stretches as far as the eye can see. Note the windows boarded-up to prevent people falling through them.

Canopy-top view of the showground.

Craghead banner, the front of which depicts David triumphant over Goliath. The motto reads: 'He that would be free must strike the blow.' The preacher that day was the Revd J. McManners, the first nonconformist to preach at the miners' service.

The Prime Minister, the Rt Hon Clement Attlee, the Rt Hon Aneurin Bevan MP, Minister of Health, the American Ambassador, Mr W. Averell Harriman, the Mayor, Councillor J.L. Robson, civic leaders and guests leaving the Market Place, after a civic reception in the Town Hall. They were walking to the castle where they had dinner, which was provided by Lyons' Café.

Approaching the Castle from Palace Green. Jack Harrison, sword-bearer, leads the dignitaries towards the castle entrance.

1947

The footpath below Pelaw Wood, February 1947. The old ash tree at the end of the railings was where the Durham Regatta races started. The once overgrown pathway to Old Durham Gardens has recently been resurfaced to make it more accessible. The photograph shows Mrs H.M. Webster and her daughter Hilary.

The old iron Baths Bridge, February 1947. This was the second bridge and was erected in 1894; it had replaced an earlier wooden bridge of 1855. The present bridge was opened in 1962.

The Galilee Chapel, Durham Cathedral, being swept by two of the cleaners, February 1947. It took these ladies a week to complete the task of sweeping the whole cathedral.

The Durham 'Hello Girls' who were operating the switchboard at the telephone exchange in the General Post Office in Claypath, February 1947. They were then taking about 12,000 calls a day; five men worked the night duty.

Staff working in the repair room at Lynch's radio shop, 30 North Road, April 1947.

Sherburn Road Youth Centre, Junior Football Team, March 1947. Back row, left to right: John Flowers, Dick McCormack, J. Carr, J. Hurst, Jack Sutherland, Jack Birch, Jim Jordan and T. Stenard. Front row: P. Hanley, G. Marley, L. Balmer, E. Kirby and J. Lake. In June that year it played a German POW team and was charged with playing on a Sunday by the Durham FA. This was illegal for registered players, and the team was suspended for two months.

Veteran runners burning up the track at the Easter Races on The Sands, 7 April 1947. The winner (left) was T.H. Fenwick. On the right is Jack Hilton (aged 79) who had won 11 races over the last 15 years; he is wearing the same running shoes he had used on the track for the last 40 years.

Mr A. Pitt of Ushaw Moor (an older runner) was given an extra start in the young men's Easter Race on The Sands, 7 April 1947.

The Durham High School playing field, originally Paradise Gardens (now part of the site of the Prince Bishop Shopping Centre), May 1947.

Cheery folk at The Sands, Easter Fair, 7 April 1947.

Children from Western Hill School at the opening of their annual concert, May 1947. The picture was taken next to the Obelisk in the grounds of St Leonard's RC School.

Lyon's Café, Silver Street, 23 May 1947, showing the ancient staircase. This property was once the town house of Sir John Duck, Durham's Dick Whittington, built c.1658. Later it became the Black Lion Hotel, then Caldcleugh's Ironmongers, and finally a café. The building was demolished in 1963 and replaced by a modern structure.

Mr Marshall, 'Cumberland Jack', enjoys a few moments outside his former home in Framwellgate, May 1947. It is interesting to see the stone foundations of an earlier building.

Mr Erik Brown, left, of Brown's Boathouse, presenting to the Regatta Committee a handsome cup in memory of his father, the late Mr Joseph Brown, June 1947. Erik's father had been the official university boat-builder since c.1903.

Police competing for the Durham County Constabulary Golfing Trophy at Mount Oswald Golf Course, Durham, 9 June 1947. Competitors were Assistant Chief Constable J. Wright, Inspector H.W. Coyne, Supt. T.R. Hammond, Inspector J.J. Hugill, , PC H. Ross, PC R.M. Collinson and PC.Carr.

The funeral service of the Mayor, Councillor F. Foster, at St Cuthbert's Church, 28 May 1947. The cortège was led by a detachment of Durham County Constabulary. The Mayor's bodyguard and officers from the city council followed Councillor Foster had a long and distinguished career in the County Constabulary and entered the local council within a year of his retirement from the Police Force, about 1940.

Brandon Colliery Welfare Flower Show and Sports Show, 30 August 1947, showing 'Zulu Warrior', Fred Hayton, of Brandon Colliery, and an unidentified 'old soldier', leading the procession. The show was attended by about 7,000 people. One of the events was a fancy dress parade with £1 being given to the person causing the most fun on the route.

The presentation of the Durham County Press Cups by Mr Arnold Rowntree at Durham Town Hall, 5 September 1947. Mr Charlton, Wheatley Hill, received a cup for the best display of chrysanthemums and the allotment cup; also the trophy for the best collection of vegetables, on behalf of Thornley Allotment Society. The cup for best display of honey went to Teesside Beekeepers' Association.

Above and below: Spectators in the Market Place at the students annual 'Rag', June 1947. Note the old Police Box and granite setts.

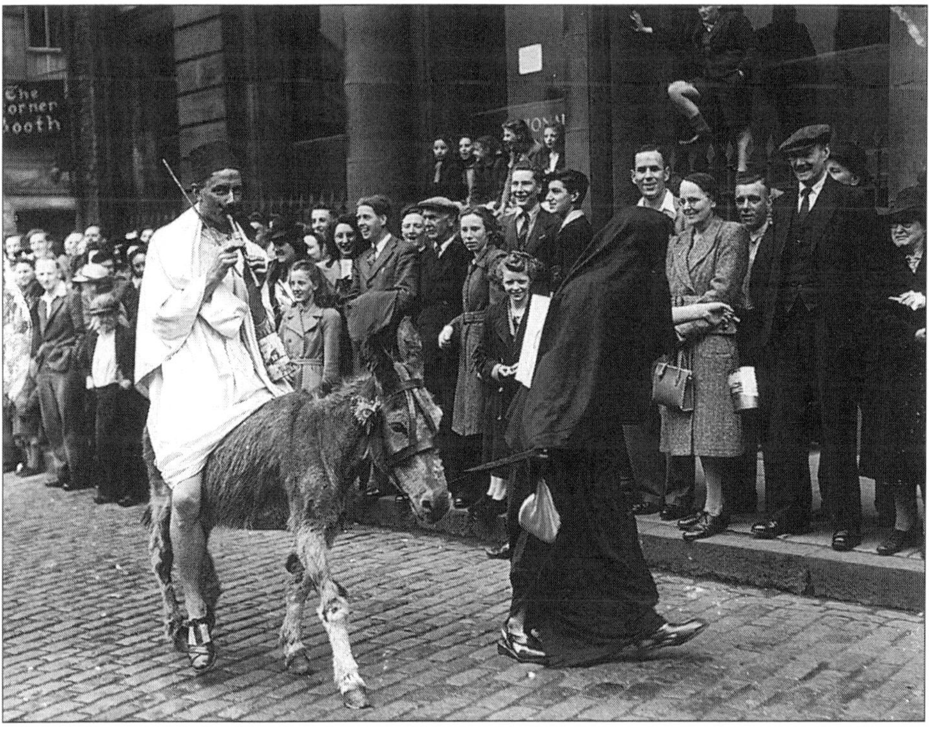

145

Durham Wasps, ice hockey team, October 1947. Back row, left to right: Bill Britt, senior (Secretary), Joe Stephenson (Ferryhill), Russ Proudfoot (Ferryhill), Geordie Belmore (Darlington), Jim Hall (Hetton-le-Hole), Chips Vine (Leamside), Bob Sandcaster (Gateshead), Bob Thompson (Bearpark), Butch Cartwright (Pity Me), J.J. Smith (Rink Manager) and Bob Bruin (Whitley Bay). Front row: Bill Britt, Junior, George Gibson (Darlington), Flash Lynn (Leamside), Earl Carlson (Darlington) and Mike Davy (Coach). The photograph was taken prior to the first British Ice Hockey International Match between an English and Scottish team. The Wasps played Kirkcaldy Flyers, the score being 5-4 to Kirkcaldy.

The visit of Princess Elizabeth, 23 October 1947. This was her first visit to the city. She was here to lay the foundation stone for St Mary's new college. She began her journey to the college after visiting the Cathedral

The Army recruitment office, 78 Claypath, December 1947. Now converted for student accommodation.

26 July 1947 - Miners' Gala

Gala speakers
Rt Hon Ernest Bevin MP, Foreign Secretary; the Rt Hon Herbert Morrison MP, Lord President of the Council; Michael Foot MP; Mr A.L. Horner, General Secretary of the NUM.

Cathedral service
Preacher: The Rt Revd Dr Alwyn Williams, The Lord Bishop of Durham.
Brancepeth Colliery Band, bandmaster Mr J.W. Wright.
Dean and Chapter Colliery Band, bandmaster Mr J. Graham.
Thornley Colliery Band, bandmaster Mr E.G.T. Kitto.
Mayor: Councillor H.C. Ferens.

Historical Notes
1 January
'Vesting Day', *ie* Coal industry nationalised. There are 108,291 men employed at 127 Durham collieries.
9 February
Explosion at Derwent Colliery, three lives lost (W. Watson, F. Monaghan and R. Heighway).
22 February
The Miners' Memorial unveiled at Evening Prayer, Durham Cathedral, by The Bishop of Durham.
20 March
Explosion at East Tanfield Colliery, one life lost.
3 July
Watergate Colliery, two lives lost (H. Morgan and W.A. Hopper).
22 August
Explosion at Louisa Old Pit, South Moor, 21 lives lost (H. Talbot, A. Bailey, E. Westgarth, J. Estell, T.M. McKeever, W. Roe, F.E. Martin, T.W. Appleby, J. Rowland, G. Moore, W. Reed, T. Bell (no.1), J.S. Hodgson, T. Bell (no.2), N. Fenwick, J. Chapman, C. Simpson, R.L. Brown, J. Grimley, W. Rutherford and R.W. Birtle).
18 September
Inundation (flooding) at Lumley 6th Colliery, two lives lost (G.E. Watson and W. Nelson).
December.
Dunston and Elswick collieries cease production.
The Durham County Brass Band League Championship was won by Shildon London and North Eastern Railway Band.

Four 'sunflowers' are captured by the photographer.

An afternoon snapshot. The bandsman has exchanged hats with one of his lady companions. His hat carries the initials 'W.H.B.' Possibly Wheatley Hill Band.

An early morning scene in the Market Place. Thornley banner is on its way from Claypath to Saddler Street. Note the old police box. Taken by Joseph March.

Late morning (11.45am by Bramwell's clock) and the last banners are seen in the distance, entering Old Elvet. The *Durham County Advertiser* reported that the attendance of 150,000 was, however, less than that of the previous year. Taken by Joseph March.

Great Expectations. The young man in the centre sports a hat with the motto: 'Kiss me quick'.

'All smile, please, for the camera.' This was the title for the picture which shows a young girl getting in some practice. Many bands welcomed girls as players.

A village mascot, in her homemade costume, prepares to strike up a note. After the war years, a number of banners were led in by such mascots.

A father tells his daughter that she is not too old for a balloon.

Two jolly young couples smile for the camera and fail to attract the attention of the serious men walking by.

Mid-afternoon, relaxing on the riverbank after the picnic lunch.

An old miner, sporting his white muffler and smoking his clay pipe, tells a likely tale to the amusement of the ladies.

A father entertains his young son with a balloon after a tour of the showground.

Three ladies powdering their faces, to the amusement of the photographer. The wording on their fancy bonnets reads (left to right): 'I'm a cuddlesome baby', 'I'll have to ask me mum', and 'What a smasher'.

A young couple take their turn at guarding the instruments. These were the prized possessions of the bandsmen.

Two miners dance to the delight of the spectators. This was one of the many spontaneous light-hearted performances put on throughout the day.

The smartly-dressed youth of the day from Trimdon Grange congregate in front of their banner. In the centre is Bob Athey.

A plain-clothes band prepares to leave the field for the homeward trek.

The 'Chief Whip' prepares to lead out Mainsforth banner and its cheerful followers.

Hamsteels banner halts for the photographer near the old Neville Hotel (right), North Road, on the journey home. It bears the portraits of Peter Lee and A.J. Cook.

1948

Jean Dodd, aged 11, of 48 Annand Road, is seen taking part in one of the first official ceremonies on the new Sunderland Road Estate, 18 January 1948. The tree was one of several silver birches planted. The Revd Dr E.G. Pace blessed the trees and offered prayers for the work of the Gardeners' Guild. He said everyone wanted the new houses to be not only places in which to eat and sleep, but to be real homes in which to take pride.

Children walking through ruined houses at Pittington, February 1948. Villagers were campaigning for new housing developments for the population of about 1,600. Many of the houses, which were still occupied, had been condemned.

Major General C.L. Loewen CB, GOC, 50th Division, inspecting men of the 8th Battalion, Durham Light Infantry, outside the Drill Hall, at the bottom of Gilesgate Bank, prior to the arrival of Mr E. Shinwell, Minister of War, March 1948. The Minister was touring the Northern Command to encourage staff officers in the drive for expansion of the TA. Officers present were, Lieut. Col G.L. Wood, DSO, MC, and Capt P.F. Greenwell, MC.

Soldiers standing to attention outside the 8th Battalion DLI Drill Hall, March 1948. Left to right: Privates Coxon and Kennedy, Sergeant Bainbridge, DCM, Privates Forster and Harrison and Corporal.Coxon.

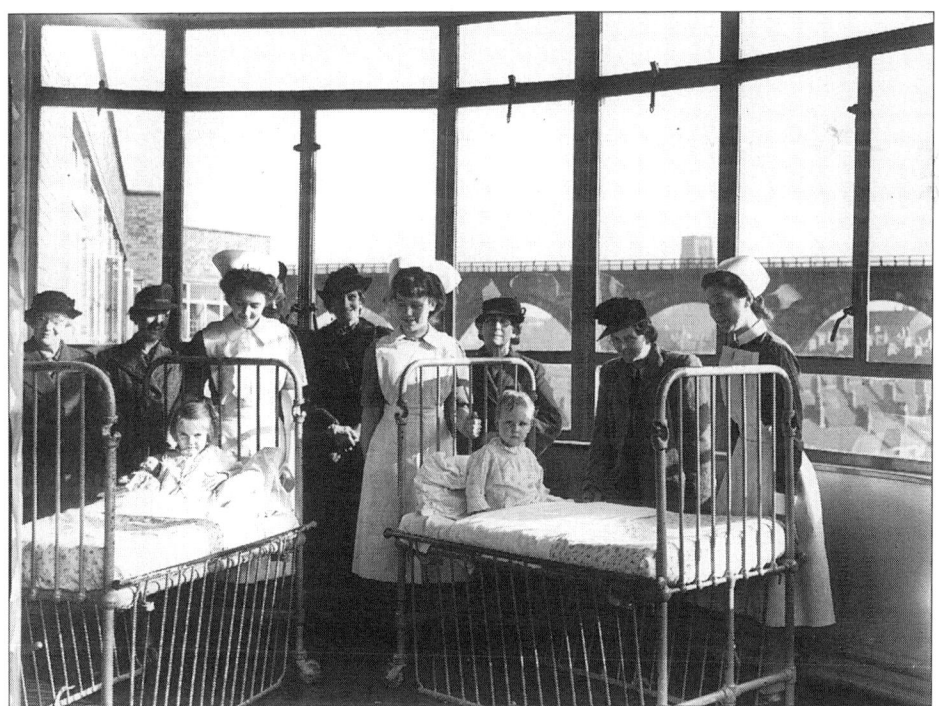

'Friends of the hospital' day at Durham County Hospital, North Road, 9 March 1948. Visitors are inspecting the new sun balcony, which was made possible by the fund raising efforts of the Friends.

Student 'Rag', Palace Green, April 1948, showing a student claiming to be a Labour MP.

Pattison's Café, Old Elvet, April 1948, now part of the Royal County Hotel.

Belmont and St Oswald's Churches held an impressive service at Finchale Priory on Ascension Day, May 1948. St Oswald's choir led the procession, the Revd C. Pickles, vicar of St Mary Magdalene, Belmont, conducted the service, and the Revd L. Lloyd Rees, Chaplain of Durham Prison, preached the sermon.

Framwellgate Moor and Pity Me Homing Pigeon Society, May 1948. Seated, in the centre, is Jack Hird, a pigeon-flyer for 41 years.

About 9,000 pigeons being released at Durham Railway Station belonging to homing-pigeon societies from many parts of the country, 22 May 1948.

Durham Horse Fair, Old Elvet, 18 May 1948, showing Norman, Kenneth and Charlie Brown being driven by their cousin, Tommy Brown.

The Women's Labour Gala procession in North Road heading towards Wharton Park, photographed with Mr Hugh Dalton, MP for Bishop Auckland, who was one of the speakers, 5 June 1948.

Members of the Church Lads' Brigade on their way to the cathedral for their annual service, June 1948, photographed passing the Durham County Hospital, North Road.

The official opening of Langley Bridge Milk Factory, 4 June 1948. The Milk Marketing Board built it on a one and half acre site; it took nearly four years to build and equip. Milk was pasteurised here at a rate of 2,000 bottles an hour.

Father Meagher, conducting the opening service at Durham ice-rink, on the occasion of the second post-war Roman Catholic Gala, 2 August 1948. Between 4,000-5,000 people attended from all parts of the Diocese of Hexham and Newcastle. In the afternoon a great gathering enjoyed games and Irish dancing on The Racecourse.

Army Cadets, Air Training Corps and Sea Cadets outside the cathedral after their annual church parade, 26 September 1948.

Sea Rangers from Durham High School and St Oswald's Church attending the launch ceremony of their boat SRS *British Princess*. The Mayor, Councillor H.C. Ferens, seen at St Cuthbert's landing stage, christened it with lemonade, 8 October 1948. The crew consisted of Minnie Cook (coxswain), Pat Forgan, Madeleine Brown, Jean Urquart, Audrey Stobbs and Kathleen Surtees.

Many of the prize-winners belonging to Durham Commercial College, Victoria Terrace, photographed after receiving their awards at the speech day ceremony held in the Town Hall, November 1948.

Men making jackets as part of a tailoring course at Finchale Rehabilitation Centre, November 1948.

Father Christmas makes a special appearance at a party arranged by Durham Police, December 1948.

24 July 1948 - Miners' Gala

Gala speakers
The Rt Hon Hartley Shawcross KC, MP, Attorney General; the Rt Hon Sir Stafford Cripps KC, MP, Chancellor of the Exchequer; Rt Hon Aneurin Bevan, MP, Minister of Health; Mr A.L. Horner, General Secretary of the NUM.
Cathedral service
Preacher: The Revd R.A. Beddoes, Vicar of Easington Colliery.
Harton Colliery Band, bandmaster Mr Jack Atherton.
Easington Colliery Band, bandmaster Mr William Delson.
Thornley Colliery Band, bandmaster Mr E.G.T. Kitto.
Mayor: Councillor H.C. Ferens.
Historical Notes
1 April
The electricity industry was nationalised.
April.
Shield Row Drift and the Grange Colliery, Carrville cease production.
June.
Introduction of the NCB Scholarship Scheme.
11 June
Explosion at Sherburn Hill Colliery, four lives lost (F. Hodgson, T.L. Philipson, R. Brown, H. Cowan).
5 July
The introduction of the National Health Service.
October.
Tanfield Moor Colliery ceased production.
December
Gift of the Production Banner to DMA by the firm of Tutill, to be competed for each year.
The Durham County Brass Band League Championship was won by Craghead Colliery.

The Racecourse from Bede College, showing Whinney Hill School in the centre of the skyline. Mr Bevan had said in his speech to the miners that Labour needed 20 years in Government to put Britain back on her feet. Taken by Mr D.E. Webster.

Early morning, and Kimblesworth banner is seen moving across Framwellgate Bridge. Note the old Criterion on the left.

Monkwearmouth banner leaving for home. It portrays a split design showing (1) a miner leaving home to go to work (entitled 'The Last Good Morning'), and (2) his widow seeking aid (entitled 'We Claim Compensation').

Home time, 3.30pm, Elvet Bridge. Usworth banner, showing the portrait of J. Keir Hardie (1856-1915) who was the first Labour MP. He has spoken at the Gala in 1905, 1906 and 1910.

The time is now 3.40pm and looking at this picture it is easy to believe the estimated attendance figure of 250,000, which made it the biggest Gala yet.

At 3.47pm, a band halts at the Magdalen steps and plays a tune, to allow the vast numbers in front of them to proceed. The banner in the distance shows a Biblical scene of Christ walking on the sea.

The homeward-bound miners and their families struggle through Saddler Street towards the Market Place. Many of the onlookers have caught sight of the photographer in his prominent vantage point.

Two mounted policemen clear the way along North Road for the homeward procession. The policeman on the right is Frank Close, of Pittington.

Veronica Hughes and her boyfriend, Thomas Brown, of Elvet, on the showfield. Durham people took advantage of the presence of this attraction on the eve of the Gala, when prices of fairground rides were reduced.

1949

A walking race from Coxhoe to Durham, 6 February 1949. The two competitors were Walter Salisbury and Jack Simpson. Simpson had a head start of two miles, moving off from the Hare & Greyhounds, Bowburn. Salisbury, who was the more experienced, won by five minutes; he is seen here entering New Elvet.

Mr Hugh Gaitskell, centre, Minister of Mines, with Mr J.D. Murray, MP accompanied by NCB officials on a visit to Brandon Pit House Colliery, March 1949. The minister had descended the shaft and crawled on his stomach to an 18" seam to talk to men at the coal-face. He wanted to see for himself the working conditions of the mine.

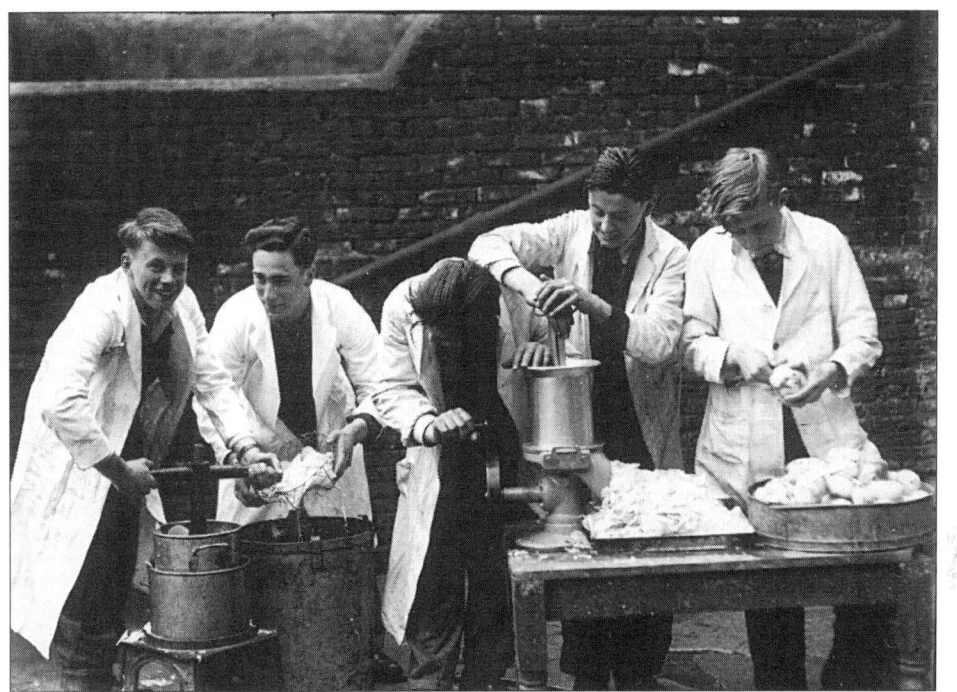

The 4th Durham (Gilesgate) Scouts on their 'Bob-a-job' tasks, assisting in the production of potato crisps. Baby-minding is performed by Jimmy Harris, April 1949. A total of £21 18s 5d was raised

Durham County Fire Brigade on parade at The Sands, Durham, 23 May 1949. Twenty-six stations from the County took part and over 200 personnel assembled for the visit of HM Inspector of Fire Services, Mr P.P. Booth. The open space in the centre of the photograph is now the site of council flats.

John Pilkington from Gilesgate holding the pigeon, which won the Deerness Valley Federation Race from Brussels, June 1949.

A baptism ceremony at Finchale Abbey attended by several thousand young and old 'Ambassadors of Christ' (Pentecostal Church Assemblies of God. Many folk had made a pilgrimage to this sacred spot from all over the country by taxi, car, bicycle, bus and on foot, Whit Monday 6 June 1949. The ceremony was organised by Pastor N. Humphries of Houghton-le-Spring. Pastor Humphries and E.J. Shearman of Willington conducted the baptisms. Mr Joseph Speed of Newbottle, also known as 'Silver King' because of the colour of his hair, is seen before he went under the water. He told the crowd that his pipe and baccy were going with him and he would never smoke again.

Miss Gladys Coates of Durham School of Dancing, Mountjoy, with her pupils on the lawn of Bede College prior to their taking part in a display of dancing, 2 July 1949. One of her former pupils was the Prime Minister, Tony Blair. Miss Coates trained as a teacher of dancing in Newcastle and started the Durham School of Dancing in 1934-5. Her studio was built by her father, the builder, Tom Coates. She married Tommy Blair in 1940, and continued to use her maiden name for teaching purposes. From 1975 she was helped by her daughter, Jennifer, who continued to teach ballet, although the studio was closed when Miss Coates died in 1996.

George Bennett & Albert Wood in *Ice Capers* a spectacular show on ice, staged at Durham Ice Rink, 22 August 1949

The opening of the 100th house at Sherburn Village by Councillor F. Kidd, Chairman of the Rural Council. The tenant was Mr G. Wilson of Pittington, 10 August 1949.

Prize winners at Bluecoat School, Claypath, December 1949.

Durham City & District Bee Keeping Association's exhibit, which had gained a cup at the County Press & Houghall Show, September 1949. Houghall Show began in the 1930s during the depression, when thousands of miners were out of work. It was first held at Dryburn. After World War Two the *Durham County Press* established their own show in the Town Hall. The first joint show was held in 1948.

Remains of an ancient clock believed to date from around 1750, which was found by Mr W.W. Cope of Messrs G. & F. Cope of Nottingham in a small circular tower overlooking the quadrangle of Durham Castle, November 1949.

Mine host Mr Jack Fallon (with the tray), at The Station Hotel, Leamside, photographed among his friends on his last night behind the bar, 28 November 1949. Those present were: Joseph Gibson, Tommy Peat, Charles Trott, Dick Harrison, E. McIlwraith, W. Morley, G. Gibson, Billy Kelly, W. Robinson, T. Storey, J. Appleby, F. Russell, W. Anderson and Bob Peebles.

Alderman J.W. Pattinson, JP (left), with some of the old folk of Elvet and Houghall, to whom he and Mrs Pattinson made an annual gift, December 1949. Alderman Pattinson was born in the city and educated first at the Wesleyan Day School and then later at the Bluecoat School. For about five years he was a footman at Durham Castle and Hatfield Hall. Later he became the proprietor of the Dunelm Hotel, Old Elvet. He was also a prominent soldier with the City Corps of the Salvation Army.

Aerial view of the city, c.1950.

Participants in the Junior Contest of the Durham County Brass Band League, Junior Contest, which was, held at Gilesgate Welfare (Vane Tempest Hall), 1949. Photographed outside the old main entrance

23 July 1949 - Miners' Gala

Gala speakers
The Rt Hon Clement Attlee, CH MP, Prime Minister; the Rt Hon Ernest Bevin MP, Foreign Secretary; the Rt Hon Herbert Morrison MP, Lord President of the Council; Mr Hugh Gaitskell, Minister of Fuel and Power and Mr A.L. Horner, General Secretary of the NUM.

Cathedral service
Preacher: The Rt Revd W.H. Baddeley, The Lord Bishop of Whitby.

Blackhall Colliery Band, bandmaster Mr Harold Laycock.
Thornley Colliery Band, bandmaster Mr E.G.T. Kitto.
Boldon Colliery Band, bandmaster Mr H. Bradley.

Mayor: Councillor J.M. Herring.

Historical Notes
The first competition for the Production Banner was held. It was won by East Tanfield Colliery.

26 April
The National Coal Board (NCB) receives its own coat of arms.

1 May
The gas industry nationalised.

May 6.
Inundation (flooding) at Thornley Colliery, three lives lost (M. Purvis, W. Rudkin and W. Kelly).

July.
Burnhope Colliery ceased production.

The Durham County Brass Band League Championship was won by Hetton Silver Band.

The Production banner, won by East Tanfield Colliery enters The Racecourse for the first time. It had been made and presented by the firm of Tutils in July 1948. It was competed for annually and awarded to the colliery which had tried the hardest to increase production.

The first banner of the day, that of Mainsforth Colliery, preceded by the officials, makes a dignified entry. It shows the aged miners' homes, Peace Haven, Ferryhill. The gentleman on the right in the light suit is Peter Davies.

South Moor No.1 banner arriving, followed by South Moor No.2.

Mrs Bowie with her husband leads in Chester Moor banner on the occasion of her 50th Gala. The black rosettes attached to the banner signify a death in the pit.

Morpeth Highland pipe band at the head of Washington Glebe miners. The hiring of Scottish pipe bands was due to the shortage of colliery bands. The band leader, a veteran of World War One, proudly wears his medals.

The young men and women follow their banner. Names in the group are Jack Harker, Fred Ryans, Tommy Foster, Ron Liddle, Dorothy Hutchinson, Ronnie Prudhoe, Don Smith, George Harker and George Liddle.

The Dawdon 'beauties', Sam Hughes (left) and Billy Wood, lead their colliery band.

High-spirited young folk compete for attention.

Three young men let off steam to the amusement of the nearby policeman.

One of the speakers, Mr Hugh Gaitskell (1906-1963) Minister of Fuel and Power. He became a socialist during the 1926 General Strike.

Herbert Morrison (right), Mr E. Moore, President of the NUM Durham Area (centre) and Arthur Horner (left), General Secretary of the NUM, on the speakers' platform. Alf Horner had said in his speech that although the miners were critical of some aspects of nationalisation, they would never under any Government go back to the old days of private ownership. The alternative to nationalisation would be economic death.

Brandon's banner seen at its first appearance on The Racecourse. Back row: Mrs Argument, not known, Billy Robinson, Ethel Robinson and Tommy Robinson. Middle row: June Argument, Ivy Lister, not known, Mrs Smith and George Hewitt. Front row: not known, Edith Argument and Norman Robinson. Taken by Mary Robinson.

Sitting proudly in front of Brandon's new banner. Left to right: not known, Derek Argument, Mrs Mary Robinson, Billy Robinson, June Argument (child), Mrs Argument and Mrs Smith

All the people with Mainsforth banner collect together in front of the speakers platform for a memorable group photograph. The bass drum records the Silver Band's formation in 1909.

The community of Eden Colliery assembled in front of their banner.

Burnhope Colliery banner. Despite the smiling faces the day was tinged with sadness due the the news of the closing of the colliery. The other banner is that of Houghton Colliery.

A banner, showing the cathedral, attempting to make its way through the Market Place, which is packed to capacity. The *Evening Chronicle* newspaper office is situated behind the banner.

The banner of Crook Drift, known as the 'Hole in the Wall' Colliery, heads towards Silver Street.

Crookhall banner leaving the Market Place into Silver Street. It shows Conishead Priory, the miners' rehabilitation centre which was opened 1930.

The unfurling of Brandon banner by Sam Watson, 9 July. The banner had been designed by Walter Lishman, art master at Durham Johnston School. The scene was taken from a photograph by Charles Hodgson showing the Victory Gala in 1946 from Pelaw Wood. Taken by Mary Robinson.

1950

Mr Charles Frederick Grey, MP (Labour) photographed after his election, with supporters and family, outside the Town Hall, 24 February 1950. Mr Grey entered Parliament in 1945 and held the seat until 1970. He was born in 1904, and started work at the age of 14 at Elemore Colliery, where he worked for more than 20 years as a coal-hewer. A native of Easington Lane Mr Grey was a miners' lodge official before 1945, and also an Independent Methodist preacher.

Mackay's football team photographed before it was defeated 2-0 in the final of the Tudhoe Orphanage Cup at Spennymoor, April 1950. Back row, left to right: Walter Shea, Fred Wharton, Tommy Little, Bobby Noble, Jack Wade, Billy Wardle and Wilf Helm. Front row, left to right: Joss Milburn, Charlie McArdle, Jimmy Crampton, George Wood and Bob Bell.

Sir Robert Chapman DL took the salute when 3,000 Boy Scouts attended a St George's Day parade and service at Durham Cathedral, 23 April 1950. The Bishop of Jarrow, the Revd J.A. Ramsbotham, preached the sermon.

The Galilee Chapel, Durham Cathedral, showing members of the Durham County Fellowship of Religion, prior to their presentation of 'The Figure on the Cross', 13 May 1950.

Rogation Day procession from St Oswald's Church, May 1950. It is seen winding its way through Thorndyke (also known as Klondike) Allotments where the crops were blessed. The procession is led by Crucifer, Mr F. Kny-Jones. This area is now part of the university science site on Stockton Road.

One of Durham's young dancing instructors, Pauline Chamberlain, with her pupils after a display in the Town Hall, 17 May 1950. Pauline was 17 years of age when she opened her dancing school in 1947 and it continued until she retired in 1970.

The new Chancellor of the University of Durham Dr G.M. Trevelyan (third from the right) leads the procession from the castle to the cathedral, with Sir James Duff (second from the right), May 1950.

Mr L.O. Duncan, a Somerset journalist, and his wife, were on a caravan tour of Great Britain, June 1950. They are photographed visiting Durham where they were met by the Mayor, Councillor H.H. Rushford, and Miss Gwen Wilkinson, (representing the RSPCA). The caravan was drawn up in the grounds of Durham Moor Farm. While on the journey, Mr Duncan was writing a book about his adventure.

Members from Neville's Cross Social club outside the club, prior to their outing to Bamburgh and Seahouses, 25 June 1950.

Odd-job man, Thomas Robinson, aged 70, a retired builder's labourer, photographed pointing the boundary wall of the bowling green which he had built at Gilesgate Welfare (Vane Tempest Hall), July 1950.

The Gilesgate Welfare Association Friendly Circles' first birthday, at Vane Tempest Hall, July 1950. Miss Moore, aged 83, cuts the cake, watched by the vicar of St Giles's, Canon Jack Norwood.

The Shakespeare Band's 'big drummer' keeps time as his colleagues entertain spectators at Durham City AFC's, first home game. The match took place on The Racecourse, 2 September 1950.

Boer War veteran, Tommy Nevison of Bishop Auckland, taking aim, at the Durham Light Infantry Association's reunion which was held at Brancepeth Castle, 31 September 1950. This was the 17th annual reunion of the DLI Regimental Association.

The 'Free Orchard' near The Sands, October 1950. Officials discussing plans for the new sports stadium for Durham City AFC, which was to be built on the site. Members of the group are: left to right: J.P. Carswell (assistant secretary), Walter Stones, B. Caldcleugh, Jack Holloway and Raymond Appleby (chairman).

Mr Justice Hallett (right) and Mr Justice Finnemore attending a service at the cathedral with the Mayor, Councillor Mrs H.H. Rushforth, and members of the Corporation, 22 October 1950. Also in the group are Dean Alington (rear left) and Mr J.K. Hope, Recorder (front left).

The master of the Durham County Foxhounds, greeting children near Shincliffe School, at the beginning of a meet, November 1950.

Flooded bus-stands when the Wear broke its banks in Framwellgate, November 1950. The young boy is Robert Howe. Note the bus going over Framwellgate Bridge.

A brightly-painted bus belonging to the Express Omnibus Co. (Durham) Ltd., Palace Green, November 1950. The firm was established at Gilesgate Moor in the 1930s.

Youth organisations of Durham Division Salvation Army demonstrating their activities at an exhibition in Durham Town Hall, 2 December 1950. More than 500 young soldiers crowded into the Town Hall.

A Christmas party at Millburngate Nursery School, December 1950. The building stood on part of the site of 'The Gates' shopping centre.

Sorting the Christmas post at Durham Post Office, Claypath, December 1950. The post office building was opened in 1929, after the one in Saddler Street closed. It has now been converted into private apartments.

A magician pulls a rabbit out of a hat for children at a Christmas party organised by Durham Police, December 1950.

22 July 1950 - Miners' Gala

Gala speakers
The Rt Hon Sir Hartley Shawcross KC, MP, Attorney General; the Rt Hon Aneurin Bevan MP, Minister of Health; the Rt Hon E. Shinwell MP, Secretary of State for War; and Mr A.L. Horner, General Secretary of the NUM.

Cathedral service
Preacher: The Rt Revd John Alexander Ramsbotham, Bishop of Jarrow.

Thornley Colliery Band, bandmaster Mr E.G.T. Kitto.
Brancepeth Colliery Band, bandmaster Mr H.M. Hardy.
Lingdale Miners' Colliery Band, bandmaster Mr F. Ramage (with Roddymoor Colliery banner).

Mayor: Councillor Mrs H.H. Rushford (first woman Mayor of Durham).

Historical Notes
February.
Miners' National Fatal Accident Fund Agreement. Re-election of Labour Government.

11 July
Hetton Lyons Colliery, Hetton-le-Hole, ceased production.

July.
Kimblesworth Colliery was Production champion.

19 October
Hugh Gaitskell took over as Chancellor of the Exchequer from Sir Stafford Cripps who was retiring on health grounds.

24 October
Explosion at Etherley Dene Colliery, one life lost (J.E. Wright).

December.
Littleburn Colliery, Langley Moor, ceased production.

The Durham County Brass Band League Championship was won by Craghead Colliery band.

National Association of Colliery Overmen, Deputies and Shotfirers banner at its first unfurling in John Street, Durham City.

Mr R.W. Smith of Sherburn Village (right), who won the competition for the best design, being congratulated by Mr J.G. Sanderson, a former president of NACODS, on the morning of Gala Day. The banner shows a manager, a deputy and a miner clasping hands. Harrison's organ factory is seen on the right.

Five smart girls lead their banner over Elvet Bridge. The spire of St Nicholas's Church is visible to the right.

Crowds proceed in leisurely fashion towards Old Elvet. Brown's Boathouse appears in the top right-hand corner.

The last airing of Hetton Lyons Banner. The attached poster explains the reason why.

The 'happy couple' from Dawdon Colliery, Sam Hughes and his 'bride', Billy Wood, with their 'bridesmaid', pause outside the Waterloo Hotel for a wedding snap under the watchful eye of the law. Two of the bandsmen on the right are: John McGrath and Stan Whitwell.

The band leads Lambton banner, draped in black veiling arriving on to The Racecourse. It carries the portrait of A.J. Cook.

Lambton supporters with their banner.

The miners and officials of Leasingthorne Colliery proudly show off their new banner (draped in black). The showfield is seen in the background.

The arrival of speakers and guests, left to right: Sam Watson, Jack Lawson, the Mayor, Councillor Mrs H. Rushford, Sir Hartley Shawcross and Aneurin Bevan. Mr Bevan spoke of the fear of another world war and said: "We say to Josef Stalin and to communist parties of the world, Let them come once more to the Security Council and ask North Korea to stop fighting."

The Mayor, Councillor Mrs Rushford, receives help with the microphone from Sir Hartley Shawcross. She welcomed the miners and their families, and introduced the speakers.

Crowds in cheerful mood listen to the speakers. Mr Shinwell, Minister for War, described the world as 'crazy' but, referring to the situation in Korea, said: "We must not allow ourselves to be stampeded into action we may ultimately regret."

A family picnic on the racecourse after the speeches. Plastic bags weren't common in those days; everything would be wrapped in newspaper.

Two young bandsmen from Easington Colliery getting in a little extra practice for the return journey.

'Played out and flat out' – mid-afternoon on The Racecourse.

'PC 49' on duty on the riverbanks. The *Durham County Advertiser* reported that the Gala had been controlled by 500 policemen, many with walkie-talkie radio sets on their backs.

Two young musicians entertain family and friends.

Going home, Bowburn Colliery banner and followers passing the Royal County Hotel. Aneurin Bevan is standing on the balcony bidding them goodbye. Attendance this year was about 200,000.

Trimdon Grange, Women's Section, Labour Party banner turning towards New Elvet, led by Lockwood Band.

Going home, Lambton banner passing the Old Elvet shops

'Flat out' – the excitement was all too much for Mr. George (Swany) Swainston. After a few pints of beer he decided to take a nap in a quiet lane off Saddler Street near the Magdalen Steps.